HELP YOUR CHILD
with
Reading & Writing

HELP YOUR CHILD

with

Reading & Writing

A PARENTS' HANDBOOK

LESLEY CLARK

Headway · Hodder & Stoughton

Cataloguing in Publication Data is available from the British Library

ISBN 0-340-60768-8

First published 1994
Impression number   10 9 8 7 6 5 4 3 2 1
Year   1999 1998 1997 1996 1995 1994

Typeset by Rowland Phototypesetting Limited, Bury St Edmunds, Suffolk.
Printed in Great Britain for Hodder & Stoughton Educational, a division
of Hodder Headline Plc, 338 Euston Road, London NW1 3BH by
Cox and Wyman Limited, Reading.

Positive Parenting

Positive Parenting is a series of handbooks primarily written for parents, in a clear, accessible style, giving practical information, sound advice and sources of specialist and general help. Based on the authors' extensive professional and personal experience, they cover a wide range of topics and provide an invaluable source of encouragement and information to all who are involved in child care in the home and in the community.

Other books in this series include:

Talking and your child by Clare Shaw – a guide outlining the details of how speech and language develops from birth to age 11 and how parents can help with the process.

Your child from 5–11 by Jennie and Lance Lindon – a guide showing parents how they can help their children through these crucial early years, stressing the contribution a caring family can make to the emotional, physical and intellectual development of the child.

Your child with special needs by Susan Kerr – a guide for the parents of the one-in-five children with special needs, giving families practical advice and emotional support, based on the shared experiences of other parents.

Help your child through school by Jennie and Lance Lindon – a guide which looks at the school years from the perspective of the family, showing how parents can help their children to get the most out of their years at primary school and how to ease the transition into secondary education.

Help your child with maths by Sue Atkinson – a comprehensive guide to show parents how they can help develop their children's mathematical awareness and confidence from babyhood through the primary years and into secondary school.

Help your child with a foreign language by Opal Dunn – a practical guide to show parents how they can re-use the techniques they used to teach their children their own language to teach them to enjoy speaking a foreign language, even if it is a language the parents do not speak well themselves.

Acknowledgements

Many thanks to everyone who helped me create this book, to the children, parents, teachers, librarians and book experts who let me snatch some of their valuable time and to pick their brains. In particular, I wish to thank the following individuals and organisations for helping me collect samples of work, quotes, surveys and insights!

Sue Bates and Jenny Blanch of the Federation of Children's Book Groups; Viv Miller and the children of Pokesdown County Primary, Bournemouth; Mike Rouse and the eleven-year-olds at The Resource Centre, Soham Village College, Soham, Cambridgeshire; Sue Ryall and her class at Wimborne County First, School Lane, Wimborne; Carol Schouten, Language Advisor, Ferndown County Middle School; Alison Small and colleagues at Hampton Junior School, Middlesex; Mrs Sparrowhawk and the children and staff of St James' CE VC First School, Gaunts Common; Sue Tipping and her class in Bournemouth; Margaret Wallen, English Advisor, Dorset Professional Education Development Service; Peter Watters, Haringay section 11 teacher.

Finally, thanks to all my family for their personal support and tolerance of the mounds of paper.

Contents

PART TWO – LEARNING SKILLS IN THE RECEPTION CLASS

PART THREE – MOVING ON: DEVELOPING EARLY SKILLS IN READING AND WRITING (Five to Seven Years)

challenges. In the classroom. At home. Pleas for the pleasures of poetry. Functional writing. Where do the rules fit in? The art of book-making.

Introduction

Setting the scene

> ❝ I was an avid reader before the children came on the scene!
>
> ❞ *(Parent with three daughters aged 7, 10 and 12)*

How I sympathise: there are never enough hours in the day. Children have busy lives and they fill our time with endless demands, delights and worries. In an ideal world there would always be room for unhurried sessions curled up with books or creating stories together. But, like you, I appreciate the need to juggle and squeeze everything into a workable routine. I know I'm biased about the importance I attach to enjoying reading and writing. This book aims to help you and your child to share the delights and to overcome some of the dilemmas as you tackle the fundamental skills.

Of course you appreciate the significance of reading and writing. They hold the key to other areas of education and play a large part in a successful future career. They are both the tools of self-expression, and a means of going beyond ourselves to explore new worlds. Whether writing a novel or a note for the milkman, reading the football results or a complex psychological thriller, the basic skills are the same. Although there is increasing media attention on methods and standards, the practical implications remain blurred.

The one message which does come across loud and clear, is how important your role is in helping your child master these skills.

It's official: Parent power works!

Research consistently shows the importance you play in your child's education, particularly in the early years. There are welcome signs that schools are working to build stronger partnerships with parents and to create effective channels of communication. We should be ready to answer this challenge.

> **❝** *I don't want to interfere with what she's doing at school.* **❞**

> **❝** *We don't want to teach her the wrong way and get her confused.* **❞**

These are fears voiced by many parents, sensitive to the professional expertise of teachers, and bemused by the different methods of teaching reading and writing. But you can offer a complimentary role, acting in partnership to support your child. If you choose not to get involved at all, you are denying her a valuable ally.

You are also ignoring your own strengths. Your positive attitude and shared enjoyment of reading and writing can be crucial to your child's success. Just think about your track record in teaching her to listen and talk, and take stock of some of the purely parental qualities you can offer:

- You know her well enough to draw upon all her real interests.
- You can tell when she is likely to be receptive, and can offer the warmth and support she needs.
- You have the freedom to show her the practical joys of reading and writing in situations which hold a personal significance for her.
- Your support and approval matter terribly to your child.
- You are her role model. If you curl up to enjoy a book and

INTRODUCTION

seem keen to catch up with your letter-writing, the chances are she'll want to do the same.

Armed with this track record, I hope you will feel confident about enjoying the language learning opportunities outlined in this book.

How to use this book

This book addresses your practical concerns about how to get involved, when to encourage and when to ease off, and where to seek advice. Most of all, it offers pleasurable experiences for you to enjoy with your child so that you act in partnership with her learning experiences at school. Whilst being positive and supportive, it acknowledges the very real concerns and problems that you and your child are likely to encounter in the struggle to master the skills of reading and writing.

Although the book follows a clear developmental sequence and gives age guides, these are only intended as a rough yardstick. The five sections of the book are designed to match broad phases in your child's education. However, your child is a marvellous individual who will mature at her own rate, follow her own interests and respond to different approaches.

As a parent whose son has just started school, I am acutely aware of the dangers of comparison and the sense of group pressure placed on parents. We all want the best for our children; we don't want to see them struggling or falling behind. Sadly, it is very easy to get sucked into a spiral of negative comparisons which can only cause unnecessary anxiety and erode your child's confidence.

Flick through the contents to find areas pertinent to your child's needs. I would also suggest that you refer to the foundation chapters to confirm the ground we're building upon.

HELP YOUR CHILD WITH READING AND WRITING

Above all, I want to promote a pleasure in reading and writing. Keep it fun as well as challenging, but keep your contact and enjoyment flowing. If you're stuck for inspiration, I hope this handbook will help, or at least guide you to those who can.

In order to include a lively range of children's writing, it has been necessary to substantially reduce the size of many samples. Although this undoubtedly detracts from their impact (and legibility), the force and variety of the work is still, I hope, a source for inspiration.

A living language, a life outside the classroom

Language foundations are laid in the home and not the school. You taught your child the value of speech, the art of conversation and listening. You share with her the fun of reading a good story and experiencing ideas through books. So you are an ideal partner to help tackle those very real challenges of learning to read and write. After all, we use words to communicate and to get information every day. You may balk at the thought of having to write an essay on your summer holidays; and the mere idea of creating a poem entitled 'seaweed' sends you to the back of the classroom! However, language is just as much about shopping lists and reminder notes pinned to the fridge door, about reading football reviews and writing holiday postcards. Instinctively you regularly show your child the practical needs for reading and writing.

From the moment you wake up, pondering over the latest free gifts on the cereal packet, your child's world is full of inviting words to explore. Every street and shop is littered with letters. Your child will be able to 'read' her favourite juice bottle label, sweet wrapper and café sign, long before she's reading books. She'll be able to tell you you're not at your usual supermarket by the colours, words and symbols around her. She'll even spot the car park and lift signs and check that you're on the right floor number.

HELP YOUR CHILD WITH READING AND WRITING

From a very early age you are introducing your toddler to a world where messages appear through signs, where drivers know what to expect because of a shared code. Our everyday world is coloured by visual messages for others to interpret. Talk about all these symbols, then get your toddler to join in a hunt for them. Road signs have a clear visual quality, as do town signs for toilets and train stations. From here progress to looking at road names, the writing on drain covers and fire hydrants and the bold lettering of shop fronts. You can even invent your own signs for hazards and highlights around the home.

It is then only a small step to the traditional pre-reading activities of labelling objects, resisting the urge to drown your belongings and loved-ones under a mountain of paper. **Purposeful pleasure** are the key words for assessing any of the suggested activities with your child. If she doesn't follow willingly, you are unlikely to have much lasting success.

As your child matures you will want to help her experience and enjoy a wide range of literature, including non-fiction and poetry. She will also need to discover different writing styles for different purposes. The practical and conversational tone of this book reflects its function. Learning the rules is important, as is knowing when and how to apply them. Make English work for your child, not just your child work for English!

First steps in talking

Why waste time talking when we all want to get down to the serious business of reading and writing? It is through conversation that your toddler begins to understand the process of communication. Only when he can express his ideas in simple sentences, and when he has a basic grounding in everyday vocabulary, can we expect him to respond to the complex tasks of reading and writing.

Talking is the starting point for his language career and you are naturally his first teacher. Your lack of formal training doesn't make conversation and listening any less important. Months of talking tirelessly to your small baby provide him with a window to the outside world, and will reap great rewards later. Research even links the early stimulus of nursery rhymes and songs to later ability in reading. You are charting out patterns and links which provide a framework for more mature skills to develop. The importance of oral communication and listening is now acknowledged in the National Curriculum. It forms the backbone of the support you give to your child as he learns to read and write.

From baby-talk to toddlers talking

Remember that first incredible moment when you became convinced that your baby was really saying something? Toddler talk is one of the real delights of parenting, with those unique baby words that inevitably mature into a barrage of questions and chatter. Like most joys, the experience will be tinged with moments of anxiety and doubt, feelings you'll encounter again and again as your child edges towards maturity as a reader and writer.

No one can say precisely how children learn to talk, read and write. What we can do is point to factors which definitely help your child develop her skills.

Early talking activities: Practical ideas to promote listening and talking

From about nine months, and even before, you'll notice that your baby takes an increasingly active role in your conversations. It's not just her eyes and limbs which show her interest, it's her responsive jingle of sounds which mirror the patterns in your talk. All conversation has pauses, changes in tone and pace, and your baby responds to the singing quality as your voice raises to ask a question or goes down at the end of a sentence. Give her time to join in and offer interpretations of her response, using gestures to show her exactly what your words mean.

Finger rhymes and gentle lap songs provide a happy introduction to sharing language. Make these sessions as animated and cosy as possible and encourage her to join in with the sounds. A sensitivity to rhyme has been shown to be a strong indicator of later reading success, so develop a love of rhymes from the start.

Once mobile, she will enjoy playing 'fetch-me' games, showing that she understands the meaning of your words. Encourage her to copy, pointing and 'asking' you to fetch teddy or asking for another drink.

Exploit toddlers' love of telephones by play-talking together, though don't look for improvement in her technique on the real thing!

When should I start reading to my baby?

Start sharing simple books and pictures early. Your baby will soon let you know if she's bored or not in the mood. Feely texture books, card books with holes and even ones which make noises, are all novelties to catch her attention. If you can add to the delights by making a little hand puppet or letting toys 'join in' the nursery rhymes, you'll enjoy yourself too!

Warning: Keep it short, sweet and simple!

Don't over-stimulate your baby. These suggestions are best tried gradually, not all at once. Turning book sessions or nursery rhymes into a floor show will confuse your baby. He won't know which stimulus to respond to first and will probably give up.

Listen hear: Talking and listening for two-year-olds

Talking and listening are intimately linked, yet we rarely teach our child how to be better listeners. You are acutely aware of the times when they fail to listen clearly, ignoring pleas to get dressed, walking in the opposite direction to the one requested or hurrying away when asked to share a toy. Selective listening starts young, but counter this with an early attempt at developing good listening habits.

Babies love playing 'find the rattle' games, turning their head in response to a noise and finding your smiling face there too. Once mobile, these noise games can take on a new dimension, particularly if you have a wind-up toy you can hide amongst the cushions or behind the chair. Hide-and-seek games have the added value of teaching your child tricky positional words ('on', 'in', 'next to' and 'under', etc.), so don't forget to tell her where the object was found.

HELP YOUR CHILD WITH READING AND WRITING

Your two-year-old will be increasing his vocabulary rapidly, and will probably already have mastered between 50 and 200 words. Give him time to test out new words, and don't discourage him by over-correcting his mistakes. He's bound to miss out the start or ending sounds of words and to get confused as to why some words are generalised (such as spoon) whilst others aren't (there really is only one Daddy!). At this stage he needs encouragement and the satisfaction of knowing that what he says is understood.

Use music to introduce a lovely range of sounds to your toddler, varying the pitch and tone of your kitchen orchestra, and leaving the musician to have a bash himself. Play games copying his sounds or trying to show the opposite of the noises he makes. He'll start to hear the contrast between fast and slow, loud and soft, high and low notes. Once you open your cupboards to this creative music making, it's surprising the variety of sounds you can create. Keep cartons which have plastic tops and fill them with different types of pasta or pulses for an instant percussion band.

Keep up the 'Fetch me' type instruction games, but make them more complex and your wishes less obvious as his skills increase. Give him the responsibility of passing on simple messages as this will help his memory too.

Sorting games are another useful way of using language, as you will also be helping him learn differences in colours, shapes and sizes. Building bricks, constructions toys and farm animals or little cars are all useful. Talk together about features that are the same, such as all the cars having wheels, then isolate something that sets them apart such as those cars which are red or which fit under your bridge.

Puppets, pictures and television also help develop his listening skills. Think how readily he responds to the jingle for his favourite programme, or how the finger puppet of a troll has him stomping around in manic monster mode. By enjoying and commenting upon a programme with your child, and regulating his television consumption, you are likely to promote rather than limit language experience.

PART 1: FIRST STEPS IN TALKING

Learning and listening skills for three-year-olds

Once your toddler goes to playgroup or nursery, there are far greater demands placed on his language skills. Teachers do not readily understand his grunts and mannerisms, so he needs to learn to use language confidently and clearly to make himself understood. He will also be expected to listen to instructions, to share experiences with other children and to enjoy stories and rhymes in a large group. Just a few seconds in a lively playgroup will show you the demands made upon fledgling listeners and talkers.

Continue using a variety of stories, action rhymes and songs to help bring out the richness and pleasures of language. The repetition of favourite stories and nursery rhymes is an important element, giving him the confidence to remember and use language. He will love it if you invent new versions of your own, particularly if they feature him as the main star. He'll also like correcting you as you make deliberate mistakes or jumble up the order of things. Don't do this too often though, and be sensitive to his desire to 'read properly' if he's not in the mood.

Children naturally start to use role-play games and show greater imagination and concentration in their play at this age. At the same time they're getting down to the serious business of practising and enhancing their language skills. You wince as your choice phrases are parroted by your toddler, urging Teddy to make haste before they're late for playgroup, or insisting hands are washed before tea! These games are far from trivial. They allow your child to explore his use of language in front of an uncritical audience. Encourage this by joining in when prompted or providing helpful props.

Introduce repetitive oral memory games. Like his favourite rhymes, this helps establish patterns in speech and improve his powers of concentration. Old favourites such as the shopping basket game, when you take it in turns to add another item to the list, can be personalised to his particular tastes and interests. Make it real by asking him to remember those special things he wanted for tea, or the toys he planned to take to his friend's house.

By this age a tape recorder is a useful aid to developing language skills. Not only will he be able to enjoy short stories and nursery music, but you can record messages and play listening lotto games. Record common sounds that you are likely to encounter during the day, from the alarm clock in the morning, to gravely footsteps on the path and the sound of dogs barking as the postman drops letters through the door. You can create an exciting mix of sounds for your child to guess at.

Having been worried by lack of vocabulary, many parents of three-year-olds suddenly find themselves overwhelmed by constant chatter and a bombardment of impossible questions. That terrifying three letter word 'why?' rears its head at every opportunity and at times leaves you feeling light-headed and breathless. Your child needs to learn that conversation is not always possible.

Being hooked on listening skills and early conversation shouldn't make you a slave to your toddler; you really don't want to talk about what he saw at the shops when you're negotiating a tricky parking manœuvre. Be honest with your child and explain why you are not prepared to listen. You won't succeed in quelling his desire to talk, but you are at least showing him how important the quality of your listening time is.

Slowly the social side of talking, of gaining attention politely and speaking in turns, should take shape. It needs your consistent response and your child's secure knowledge that there are plenty of times during the day when he is likely to get your undivided attention, for there to be any lasting impression.

Fortunately your toddler really is thirsty for knowledge, so naming new objects and experiences, using increasingly complex language to answer his questions, will help develop his own powers of expression.

Link language to his other senses by playing taste-testing games,

PART 1: FIRST STEPS IN TALKING

or describing the feel of new mystery objects then trying to guess what they are for. Exotic fruit provide a tantalising range of smells, textures and flavours to relish together.

Try creating simple books of your own. A family holiday or special outing – with the resulting collection of photos – often provides a good starting point. Let your child select and order a few pictures, then write down any caption he dictates to you. He'll take great pleasure in 'reading' the diary back to his teacher at playgroup. This can be a great prop for less confident talkers.

Now that your child is familiar with books, he will be getting some feel for the type of language used in stories, of how a sequence of events unfolds to a satisfactory conclusion. Have a go at telling rather than always reading stories. Once you've worked up the confidence, you'll appreciate how liberating and entertaining an experience it is. What's more, you'll have your toddler thirsty for a sequel, particularly if the tale features family and friends. By creating your own stories, you can adjust the pace and tension of the tale to suit your listener, adding more detail and descriptive language when he's thirsty for more. Later he can help invent scenes, sound effects and potential outcomes so that he too is really using language creatively.

Listening-to-learn: skills for four-year-olds and above

Your efforts with talking, reading and playing will continue to provide the basis for your child's development. As she matures, her range of language and the types of experiences she encounters will also increase. By five she will be like a walking dictionary, having an impressive vocabulary of about 8,000 words.

Your attention has probably now shifted to how well she uses language, and how confident she is socially. It may be difficult to judge this without spending some time talking to playgroup leaders.

Listen to how she starts or responds to casual conversation with other children in the playground, and her chatter as she plays with friends at home.

❲ *Me want kell you somefin!* **❳**

You may feel anxious about mistakes she keeps making in pronunciation or grammar rules, but most problems will resolve themselves naturally as she matures. Errors with tenses and plurals are very common, as your child has to discover irregularities in the general rules she has learnt. This is rather like the pitfalls in spelling which she will discover in writing. You can help her by offering the correct version, whilst not stunting the flow of conversation or her confidence by going overboard. If she has a particular difficulty, you might be lucky enough to find a good story or rhyme which offers the words in an enjoyable context. She won't mind hearing these again and again, and will probably pick up the correct pattern of speech in the process.

❲ *Don't touch the wadigator. It's hot!* **❳**

Difficulties with pronunciation are harder to assess. There is nothing worse than well-meaning friends asking you whether you're having your child's speech 'defect' seen to. This is guaranteed to put you on the defensive and raise anxiety levels.

It's almost as hard to tackle friends who laugh at your child's pronunciation. We're all prone to enjoying the cuteness of toddler talk and it's tempting to mimic their phrases almost as a sign of affection. But this holds the danger of making your child feel foolish, and of starting to assume that she can't say particular words correctly.

This isn't to say that you should suppress any fears you may have. It is better to seek the professional opinion of your health visitor and a speech therapist, than to let anxieties ride.

Talk to nursery staff and other adults who regularly listen to your child to gauge how difficult it is for them to understand what she is saying. You will feel more confident about your child starting school if you know that she is able to communicate happily with adults and her peers.

You may be advised to delay a formal review or correction process for minor speech problems, as your child will have a lot to contend with in adapting to school life. Your priority should be in shielding her from anxieties and inhibitions so that she is able to participate freely in class debate. It could be that the increasing emphasis on making and hearing different sounds that she is likely to encounter in reading and writing will help fine-tune her speech too.

Activities and games for fours plus

These games offer support for all of your child's first years at school too.

Increased concentration and social skills allow you to play more complex games together. Any game involves her in listening clearly so that she understands the rules and objectives. These types of listening skills are important when she starts school so that she can follow simple directions to work independently or contribute to group activities.

Use old favourites such as lotto, memory games and snap, but add new challenges, such as describing the pictures or predicting which cards are left. As she starts to understand initial sounds in words, or rhymes, adapt the rules to practise these skills.

Lotto games often provide a ready mix of pictures which can be linked and sorted in different ways. Match objects according to their function and then try to put them in a particular sequence. For example you could collect pictures of different clothes, then group them according to their warmth or purpose. Order the cards according to the pattern of the seasons or, more simply, which clothes you would put on first. Talking through such sequences helps increase her powers of expression and observation.

Use music and singing with older children, giving them greater challenges for their listening skills. Start by getting your child to mirror a song or rhythm which you play to her. You could do this first with percussion, emphasising the length and speed of the different beats. She could then choose an instrument to play back the beat to you, commenting on the similarities and differences. Not only is she learning to distinguish different sounds, but you are also asking her to remember accurately and to comment on any changes she notices. This is very challenging, so you may be happier starting with familiar nursery rhymes. You could sing in different tones, or alter key words and encourage her to distinguish rhyming sounds at the end of words. If she shows an interest, you could write out these rhyming words and recreate them in a personalised poem or song.

Tongue-twisters, riddles and word-play activities are another enjoyable way of tapping these skills. You are free to invent, whilst savouring the similarities in sounds. Riddles are a popular and a useful way to help your child predict and then to explain the reasons for her guess. You may well be flooded with toddler-type riddles and jokes, often at inopportune times, but this is a small price to pay for her enthusiasm.

Use tape recorders to leave simple practical instructions for your toddler to follow, such as how to build a bridge or make a play dough mouse. Then reverse roles and ask her to record an activity for you to try. This is very demanding as your toddler will lack experience in sequencing, describing in detail and in not relying upon assumed knowledge. Have fun together looking at the results of her instructions. Don't neglect the tape for other creative purposes, such as inventing songs or interviewing your toddler after he's transformed himself into Banana-Boy.

This brings us back to imaginative play, role play and the influences of current fads and television. If the latter are getting her to use language in a variety of ways and with obvious enjoyment, then it's wise to stomach the side-effects.

All these activities help your child to use talking and listening as a means of both discovering new facts and consolidating what she knows already.

This chapter aims to show the connections between language skills. For a detailed analysis of talking and listening skills, let me refer you to Clare Shaw's book *Talking and your child*, also in the Positive Parenting series.

CHAPTER TWO

First steps in reading

Pre-reading at home

'Pre-reading' is an ugly phrase because it tends to undermine the value of the skills involved and to mask the importance of your role. Reading is a highly complex process containing a range of different sub-skills which your child must master before he can read independently.

The activities you enjoy together at home are no less important because they may appear to be 'just playing', or because you are not working from an official reading scheme. Without the secure foundations provided by these activities, the chances are that your child's progress in learning to read could be delayed.

Your role is central

You want to give your child the best possible start to reading, yet there is little agreement as to the best methods for achieving this goal. The drift seems to be that most children learn to read eventually (somehow), and that a range of different approaches should ensure that progress is not unduly delayed.

What research does show again and again, is how important your involvement is to your child's attitude and success in literacy. This process starts long before your child faces her first school reader.

PART 1: FIRST STEPS IN READING

Can you remember how you learnt to read? Perhaps you have vague recollections of dull reading schemes, lists of sounds to learn, tins teeming with paper words to memorise and, of course, the mighty alphabet lurking cheerfully in the background. All this seems far removed from the bouncy energy of picture books and the cosy enjoyment of your reading sessions at home. But it is through you that your child will develop a thirst for books, and your own enthusiasm really is infectious. So I make no apologies for starting back in the nursery, with the pre-school reading and games, because it is there that the seeds of learning are sown.

Don't hurry it or worry too soon

One of the dangers of harking back to our own school days is that we don't remember the complexities involved in learning to read. We have a sort of check-list mentality which assumes that simply putting the right ingredients together should ensure that our children's reading takes off. What has become for us an automatic function, is actually a highly demanding process. Yes, we can help this process along, but we can't hurry it. Your child will read when he is ready and not before.

So try different methods, experience a wide range of books and language games. But don't look for immediate results or panic when you see your friend's child reading Ladybird books in the doctor's surgery. The child who reads at three has a special need or gift which requires careful provision. Whatever your child's natural ability, the time you spend together in these early years can have a big impact upon his response to formal teaching. Most of all, you are there to encourage. Without the will to succeed and the desire to learn, your child's progress is likely to be slowed.

A guide to choosing books

A good book opens up your child's world. It confirms and reassures her own experiences and emotions, or it leads to new horizons floods her thoughts with fresh imaginative and creative delights. There are so many picture books around, often very expensive, so how do you go about creating a 'home library' to enjoy with your child? Like all of us, children are contrary beasts. What works for one child may be ignored by another, but there are general principles you can use to assess the quality and appeal of a book.

Library links

Firstly, it is never too early to create links with your local library. Many newer libraries offer feeding and changing facilities, together with soft toys and quiet play areas for toddlers. Legislation about wheelchair access should make them pushchair friendly too. Yes, libraries are about books, but they want the whole family involved. You are more likely to feel relaxed about helping your older child select a book when you know your toddler is playing with lego, not crawling under the bookshelves. You may still have to retrieve him from around the counter, but ignore the disapproving glances. These early efforts to get toddlers hooked on books are worth the effort. Library books allow you to explore without the expense, and help your toddler learn to care for books too. You can seek the advice of specialist librarians when selecting books for babies and toddlers.

Other sources of advice include playgroup leaders and nursery teachers. There are also a number of children's book clubs and societies which you could get involved with. See the appendix on page 212 for details.

Picture this! Qualities of early books

The visual appeal of books is vitally important. It is through the pictures that your child first learns the communicative function of books. He will soon be able to share in telling his favourite tales through intelligent interpretation of the pictures. Apart from this, it is the pictures which grab his attention and make him want to open the book in the first place.

First books should have bold, clear pictures without too much confusing detail and probably with very little text. You will then be able to point out familiar objects or situations and to talk through the book with your child. Board books, plastic books and excitingly-textured cloth books are also a good idea whilst your baby is literally tempted to eat them.

First books have illustrations with a lively appeal yet which focus on the familiar objects and experiences which colour your child's world. Whether in primary colours or black and white, the most successful images for babies have a bold clarity and solid quality.

Good picture books have a perfect blend between the writing and the illustrations. As your toddler moves to more detailed books, look for those which show this quality.

Many books focus on the familiar and support the experiences that your child already knows. This should encourage her to discuss the story and to draw connections with her own life. She will be able to express similarities and differences, and will learn that books have a direct, personal relevance for her.

Growing up: Choosing picture books for twos plus

As your child's concentration and general maturity develops, this should be reflected in the types of books you read together. The text will get longer, with a broader vocabulary and more descriptive language. The pictures should be more involved, perhaps offering different levels of interpretation, and they should definitely add details to the story. Try to offer a good diet of artistic styles and to mingle books which use rhyme, song, noises and additional interest (such as lift-the-flap or pop-ups) with other story books.

Toddlers need a good range of content, humour and style. They want books which excite and lead to flights of fantasy and adventure as well as those firmly focused on their everyday world. Look for books which address real fears and intense feelings as well as those dealing with more comfortable everyday experiences. A book showing that others share these strong emotions may help both of you cope with your own. Don't neglect the excellent range of very young non-fiction texts which has emerged in recent years. There are books which help your child understand what to expect from her first days at playgroup, a visit to the dentist and a trip by bus. Many factual books use stunning photos or a lively action-packed cartoon style to attract their readers and prompt questions.

Books should have a clear sequence in how they develop. This will help your child follow the storyline and remember key events. There is a great sense of satisfaction in learning how stories work and build to a strong conclusion. Older children love the element of surprise, of a shared joke. They also have a strong sense of justice, of good and evil, so the fantastical (and often cruel) world of fairy tales becomes popular.

What's she learning by just listening to stories?

We think of listening as passive. It should be relaxing and enjoyable, but that doesn't mean that your child isn't actively participating and learning at the same time. The most important lesson will still be in showing the richness and value of books, but there are more specific book-facts involved too.

Firstly your toddler will find out that books have a right way up, that you turn the pages from the front to the back to follow the story, and that you read from left to right, and from top to bottom. She won't necessarily express these observations, as she won't voice her discovery that it's the squiggles, not the pictures, which tell the story. She'll gradually come to appreciate terms such as 'page', 'cover' and 'author' and will start to show an interest in the words.

Words, letters and sentences don't mean much to your toddler, but she'll ask what a book is called, what a particular word says, and will point out connections that she makes. This may be linked to an interest in seeing and trying to write her own name. You don't want to spoil shared reading pleasures with too frequent word-attack tasks, but odd references to letters, key words and sounds should fuel her interest.

Pictures are part of reading

Talking about the pictures helps establish prediction skills. She will need to interpret what she sees, remember what she has found out already, and then make an informed guess as to possible outcomes.

Guessing and 'cheating' by looking at the pictures are not bad habits. Since we know real readers don't have to use pictures, we tend to undermine the value of pictures in getting readers started. We read because we want to make sense of what has been recorded in the book, what it says. This is exactly what your child is trying to do when she looks at the pictures.

> **❝** *She's not reading, just remembering whole passages from her favourite books.* **❞**
>
> (Parent with daughter, aged four)

Your child acts like a reader before she can actually recognise all the words. She may be able to memorise whole chunks of her favourite text, but this again is a positive rather than a negative sign.

She's experimenting what it feels like to be a reader, and gaining confidence in using books independently. If you still have any doubts about the benefits of 'play reading', just observe her next time she settles down with a book. You'll get a real glow of pride seeing her so happily absorbed. Notice the way she uses her own language to match the story she sees unfolding, adding details, animating with different voices and sound effects, even pausing for emphasis and expression. There you have evidence of just how much work has gone on in those casual story sessions, and the joy she gets out of reading.

Ready for reading: What are the signs?

There are dangers in offering a simple checklist of pre-reading skills. You naturally want some evidence that your efforts are going to help rather than confuse, and there certainly are things to look out for. However, the highly individual nature of learning makes it impossible to conclude that a mastery of these skills will automatically result in your child becoming a reader. There is usually a great deal of repetition and revision required before the pieces of this learning jigsaw fall into place. Some children seem to make these leaps towards literacy more easily than others. Keep focusing on your child's confidence and progress and what she has achieved, rather than how far she has to go.

Here are the sorts of clues which indicate your child is moving towards reading.

- She enjoys sharing reading sessions with you and readily retells her favourite stories. She will also try reading a book from memory or by using the pictures.
- She has good listening skills, and can concentrate well for short amounts of time. She hears differences in sounds and can remember simple messages.
- She has a good visual memory and is able to distinguish basic shapes, such as circles and squares. She understands terms like 'straight', 'curved', and directional language like 'next to'. She notices signs and symbols when you are out, and can detect simple sequence patterns.
- She can express her ideas clearly and has a good range of vocabulary. She is able to explain differences and similarities and to give reasons as to why one set of circumstances, such as rainy weather, might lead to another, such as muddy boots. This might seem rather odd, but her powers of deduction and analysis are important when decoding the messages

she reads in print. She must be able to detect minute differences and to make connections from the diverse information she receives.

- She has started to express an interest in reading and writing, probably by wanting you to help her write her name. She may also start to spot her personal letters in other places, such as on street signs or cereal packets. See if she can recognise her name on lists, school clothes labels or library cards.

- She enjoys construction games and jigsaws, which help develop concentration and spatial awareness, i.e. how things fit together and their relative size. When you think about the mass of squiggles which make up letters and the thousands of visual combinations which make up words, you'll appreciate the value of these skills.

- She enjoys playing with words, probably through listening to poems and nursery rhymes. She is able to add ideas of her own, showing that she can hear links in the sound patterns of the word endings. She should also like repeating rhymes and practising her creative talents.

- She should be interested in recording her own ideas, with increasingly detailed drawings and perhaps an interest in writing words of her own.

- Her questions show you that she wants to know more and that she is interested in learning to read.

You don't need all these signs to be in place before you attempt more reading-related tasks, but your child's motivation and confidence are essential for success.

What can I do to help? Early reading games and activities

Most of these games can be enjoyed by children throughout their Primary years. Just adapt the ideas to suit your child. For further inspiration, refer to the index and the Appendix on page 220.

There are plenty of enjoyable activities which will help your child both develop and practise her reading skills. This list offers a few suggestions, and you will probably find that fresh ideas emerge naturally once you get going. Children are wonderfully inventive and are not held back by practicalities like time. Between you, you should make a winning combination.

Make it match

- Develop your earlier sign-spotting games and look more closely at the form of individual letters or key words. Many kids love it when you litter your house with labels, particularly on treasured objects like televisions, bunk-beds and toothbrushes! Start with words which look very different, copy out duplicate labels and then ask your child to match them. Soon she will automatically 'read' the word without needing to check on the object. Then you can add to the list using words as similar as 'bear' and 'bed', but don't make it too difficult too soon. Your child needs plenty of time to practise and gain confidence.
- Adapt this game to make your own bingo, snap, dominoes or lotto. Start with picture clues to help her match the words: guessing intelligently is an important tool in her learning. Begin with a maximum of ten words which have clear visual clues, like 'cat', 'house' and 'baby'. Gradually concentrate

more on the visual pattern of the words for matching, before tackling the more complicated task of matching an unlabelled picture to a word.

- Noticing detail is another facet of reading, so lively spot-the-difference comic pictures or visual matching games are also useful. You can make your own by investing in two copies of her favourite comic. Then choose a detailed picture, stick one onto card as a base board and chop the other picture into individual objects which must be found in the main picture. Later you can do the same with bright captions and titles, before using individual words or chunks of text.

- Use favourite construction kits to make simple models and patterns which match exactly, as well as ones which are nearly the same. You can start by using the colour and order of her bricks, then try varying the number and type of bricks. Start very simply so that your child is encouraged by her own sense of success to do more. She can also have a turn at setting these puzzles for you: by checking your answer she is developing her own observational skills also.

- Use a small magnet tied to a piece of string as a rod by which to hook paper-clipped words on fish-shaped cards from a pool. Start by getting used to the dexterity and hand-to-eye co-ordination required, reading whatever words she manages to fish out. You can later ask her to find fish which start with the same letter, or to fish out all the words which are objects you'd find in her bedroom.

With all these matching games, draw upon the humour of mismatching and making silly mistakes. Laughing can help learning too.

Letter lovers and early alphabet awareness

- Magnetic letters are a nice way to form words and copy letter patterns without the additional pressure of writing. Invest in a couple of packets of lower case letters, and one of capitals

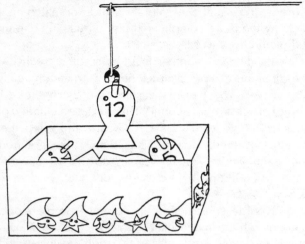

Magnetic fishing game using numbers or words.

for names, and stick them on the freezer door. Make up names and simple greetings for her to read. Later, help alphabet knowledge by putting up small sequences, getting her to match then read them. She will need to use the alphabet like a filing system, so her responses must be as automatic as possible.

Learning letters and sounds: the tools for the trade

Reading and writing is much more than learning about letters, but they do fascinate children, so get going as soon as your child gives the signal. Use puzzles, games and attractive ABC books to support her interest.

Say the sounds

Your child will have to learn both the names and the sounds of the alphabet, but the sounds and shapes of letters are a priority because they form the basic phonic knowledge needed for reading and spelling.

Our sound system is complicated, with vowels making at least two distinct sounds, and 'soft' and 'hard' variations for other letters. You can give your child a simple start by finding examples of 'pure' sounds at the beginning of words, rather than blends. In 'Smile at the sky to make the sun shine.', four words begin with the letter 's', but only one offers the sound 'ss' in isolation: 'sk', 'sm' and 'sh' all blend sounds together.

Keep the letter sounds short and accurate – for example, make sure you say *just* the hissing 's' sound from 'sun' and not 'su' or 'suh', and say a tiny, short 't', not 'tuh' to illustrate 't'. Learn through play and observation by having lively puzzles, books and an ABC frieze to enjoy. (See the Appendix on page 220 for a few examples and page 64 for further details.)

Here is a list of key words which provide correct sound clues.

'a' as in ambulance	'i' as in insects	'r' as in rabbit
'b' as in boy	'j' as in jumper	's' as in sun
'c' as in cat	'k' as in kite	't' as in telephone
'd' as in Dad or dog	'l' as in leaves	'u' as in umbrella
	'm' as in monkey or Mum	'v' as in vegetables
'e' as in egg	'n' as in necklace	'w' as in window
'f' as in fish	'o' as in orange	'x' as in fox
'g' as in girl	'p' as in paint	'y' as in yellow
'h' as in hat	'q' as in queen	'z' as in zoo

Long vowel sounds include 'a' as in 'apron', 'e' as in 'evening', 'i' as in 'ice-cream', 'o' as in 'open', and 'u' as in 'uniform'.

Relying on names to teach letter sounds is often impossible: you'd have thought I'd know better than to call my sons Sean and Ian!

Listening skills

Unless your child can hear the changes in sounds, she won't be able to take up the visual clues offered on the printed page. That is why making music, singing games and rhymes are so useful at this stage. Use a multi-sensory approach to help her make connections. You do this by saying the letter sounds as you write: seeing the pattern, hearing the sounds and feeling the handwriting flow, all at the same time.

Play I Spy games using pictures from her favourite books, or use an egg timer and count how many words starting with a certain sound she can find. The more fun and sense of anticipation you can generate, the more willing she will be to play the game. Once children understand what the game's about, and have some understanding of letter sounds, they readily create their own variations.

Keep your tape recorder handy for creating and listening to songs and poems. Relate these to her current interests, whether it's a potion for Polly Pocket, a message for Postman Pat or a spell to zap the evil Hood, your objectives will be the same! Tapes are an excellent tool for testing her memory and for introducing her to well-read story tapes. (See the Appendix on page 220).

Remember, remember . . .

Memory plays an important part in reading. There are different types of memory involved, from the more obvious recognition of the pattern of letters and words, to remembering sequences and sounds. Play games which help your child develop these skills, such as those already described in the previous chapter.

Making your own books and using words at home

Reading helps writing and vice versa. As your child starts to record her ideas this will help her reading. You are perfectly placed to offer timely suggestions about making simple books together. This could be in response to something you've read. Perhaps she wants to make her own version of *Goldilocks and the Three Bears*. Start by helping her produce a series of pictures which tell her story. Painting, sticking or making a collage will add to the appeal, as long as you can still turn the pages.

Alternatively, you could use photos from a birthday party or outing to make an album with simple captions. Discuss with your child what she wants you to write, trying to keep the sentences clear and simple. You can then put your pages in order, number them and make a bright cover with stiff card. Bind your book using a simple hole punch, staples or by sewing, ensuring the pages can be turned without tearing. You now have a real book to share with family and friends, that your child will feel confident about reading to herself or her teddies.

Encourage your child to 'write' stories of her own, then talk through and praise her work. Making your own books will highlight the need to understand the order of events. You can't make sense of a story by skipping to and fro and by muddling up the pages.

There are other ways you can combine reading and writing at home. Progress from the labelling games described earlier, to making simple notices such as 'Quiet please', 'Shoes off' and 'chocolate biscuits'. Get your child to dictate messages which are important to her such as reminders to watch her favourite programme, or requests for blackcurrant rather than orange juice when you next go shopping.

Introduce writing as much as possible in imaginative and creative

Shared story writing is fun.

play: you could make tickets for the spaceship you've just built, or write patient notes and healthy adverts for a toy's clinic.

Reading role model

If you regularly enjoy different types of books, manuals and magazines, the chances are that your child will want to do the same. If you provide her with a wide variety of books, take her to the library, point out notices and read messages, your child will want to find out more. Having games, activities and ideas to hand will make you able to respond to her interests.

CHAPTER THREE

Foundations in writing

There is obviously an overlap between early reading and writing, but when we approach writing we are also concerned with physical co-ordination and with helping our children enjoy expressing their ideas on paper. Children are highly individual. Some have an endless thirst for drawing which leads to a fine-tuning of pencil control and a desire to record their ideas. Others have to be prompted to go anywhere near a pencil. I have a son who fits into this latter category, requiring all my teacherly energy to make any pencil or craft activities seem fun. He rarely chooses to take up a crayon or paintbrush, but actually enjoys creating once he's there.

Writing requires different skills to reading, and good hand-to-eye co-ordination. Some children take far longer than others to make progress, and there are often physical reasons for this. But all can be helped with praise and enjoyable practice. At this stage your role may largely be creating opportunities for your child to enjoy drawing and play writing, coupled with focusing her attention on letters and showing her how they're written.

Exploding a myth

Even some nursery teachers perpetuate the myth that it is better to do nothing than to confuse your child by teaching her the 'wrong' approach to writing. Yes, there are many different handwriting styles, and it would be better if what you teach matches what your child will meet at school. However, as long as you focus on the start position and direction of strokes, you'll be setting an excellent example for your Little Letterer. Even if you teach capitals rather than lower case, and 'too much' copying or free writing, a happily involved child will be learning. As long as you get her holding the pencil correctly (see page 29), the fact that she's enjoying holding that pencil is worth more than the style of her lettering. If you stick to the guidelines offered on page 78, any differences can be easily corrected in her reception year. Few teachers I've met would really prefer their pupils to be a blank page to write on. If the interest is there, get going!

The participation of your child is more obvious when you are asking her to produce something, rather than to respond to a book or conversation. She must now use the observational abilities she has aquired already to develop a keener perception of print. By getting her confident and happy to produce and talk about 'scribble', you are providing the basis for her later writing career.

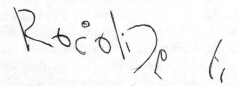

This little writer already uses some real letters and spacing.

Even with a word processor, I am very aware of how intimidating an empty page can be. How hard it is to transfer that perfect idea from mind to written matter! If it tests us adults, the problems are magnified for little fingers which demand so much concentration and energy just to ensure the pencil moves in the desired direction. Here, once more your patient parent power is invaluable in laying foundations and giving her the one-to-one attention she needs to get going.

Getting off on the write tracks: Physical skills

Co-ordination, control and concentration

Let's look first at the physical skills your toddler will need in order to be able to write, and how you can help him get started. He will have had plenty of chances to handle objects, play with building blocks and jigsaws and will have taken up the challenge of activity toys. This limbers up hand-to-eye co-ordination, and gives his fingers the chance to strengthen and tone their muscles. Staying power and concentration are two other prerequisites for writing.

Once crayons can be held and not chewed, a toddler of about eighteen months will enjoy short bursts of making his mark on the world. Your energies will be focused on ensuring these scribbles are confined to the page. Initially he will produce 'rainbows' using wide, straight-armed strokes. These will soon calm into more controlled circular movements, vertical lines and dots. Encourage all these early efforts, perhaps by sitting with him to praise, offer tips and samples of your own.

When his drawings show more detail, and some recognisable forms, he may be ready to try writing activities. Don't rush him into producing controlled patterns too early: he needs time to explore and consolidate his abilities. Children under three rarely plan their drawings; they love creating for its own sake. By being around to help make pictures, and to talk about shapes and sizes, you provide the framework for more accurate pencil work.

Early emphasis should be on free experimentation and enjoyment, but do watch how he holds his pencil or crayon and get it right from the start. Demonstrate, using the hand your child seems to prefer, guiding his fingers so they form a triangular grip about two centimetres from the tip of the pencil. His second finger should support the pencil as he grips it between his thumb and first finger. If he finds this odd and difficult, there are special corrective triangular grips, even triangular-shaped pencils, available to help.

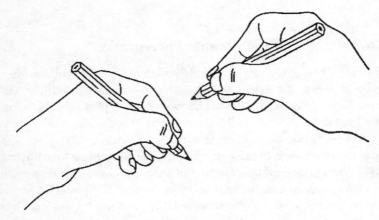

Correct pencil grip (a small child's hand).

Pencil pointers – from drawing to lettering

Before he can write individual letters, look for these refinements in your child's drawings:

- He can produce clear, strong strokes on the page, which show even pressure. This means he shouldn't be going through the paper one minute, and producing a thin spidery line the next.

- He can stop and start his pencil without letting it run away from him. Play a traffic-light type game, perhaps giving his 'pencil car' a road obstacle course. Ask him to stop and change direction when the policewoman calls out commands. This is a fun way of starting controlled pencil play activities, as he will need to keep his pencil line on the road, between two lines which you have drawn on a base board.

Start with a very simple wide road, going across the page, then add increasingly demanding bends, loops and junctions. Eventually you want him to be able to draw marks then find a suitable restarting point, just as we do when writing letters.

- He needs to copy different patterns and shapes, so dot-to-dot puzzles, mazes and colouring activities will channel these skills. If you devise your own zig-zag and looped patterns, try to create them to match his interests. From the smoke-stream of a Thunderbird rocket to the footprints of a prancing pony, the pencil power will be the same! Get him to make these marks in a left-to-right direction, so as to prepare him for the orientation of writing.

- He should have started to recognise key letters, such as those in his name, and be pointing them out to you in books, on signs and in different types of print.

For your efforts to be successful your child must be interested and eager to share in this special adult code. He must see and hear the differences in sound and pattern which will let him into these secrets.

Observing what writing is and how it works

This brings us full circle, to the efforts you make when reading together and talking. Your child needs to appreciate that the letters which say his name will do so only when put in a precise order. Letters must be accurately copied and placed to produce meaning.

His questions as you read books will allow you to explain the difference between a word and a letter and to show him similarities as they arise in a meaningful context. What you may find difficult to remember is that the distinctions between letters, punctuation marks and number symbols are really quite arbitrary and not at all obvious. Even if your child is observant and can hear differences in sound patterns, the path to writing is extremely complex.

Let him see you doodling. Then write a caption underneath and point out the words as you read together. If you encourage play

HELP YOUR CHILD WITH READING AND WRITING

You don't need to be a great artist to make exciting shapes for your child to follow!

writing from an early stage, it will reveal a great deal about what your child fully understands. Physical skills like writing may lag behind the sophistication of what he understands about reading, but the two skills are obviously interlinked.

Once he's confident about what you mean by a word, go on some of the hunts described earlier (pages xviii). Add searches which focus exclusively on print, such as exploring the contents of a comic or book and finding his favourite character's name on each page. Give him the thrill of using a bright highlighter pen on an old comic to find as many examples of the same word, such as 'teddy' on one page. This is a useful way of emphasising common words ('a', 'and', 'he', 'I', 'in', 'is', 'it', 'of', 'that', 'the', 'to', 'was', etc.) which have little meaning or interest on their own. There is a grey mass of 'joining' words which make up about a quarter of all those your child is likely to encounter in books, but which don't do anything by themselves. The quicker they are on automatic recall, the sooner fluent reading and independent spelling are likely.

As you play these games, you can point out variations in typeface and in letter sizing, whilst also showing the difference between capital and lower case. One of the added difficulties for children is in learning to ignore differences which don't change the meaning of a word, whilst looking out for those which do.

Find similarities between words, such as looking at their first sounds and letters, or noticing the same end to rhyming words. You could make families of these words and then use them to compose spells, poems and tongue-twisters. By writing down and observing together, you are introducing strategies which your child will use later to read and spell independently.

Letters present pitfalls for novices. The difference between each squiggle may be slight, but it is significant. Even if you remember the shape of a letter, you also have to decide which way round it goes. Think of 'b', 'd', 'p', and 'q', and you'll see the problem. Double the complexity by supplying a little and big version of each letter, then throw in a profusion of different typefaces for good measure. With all these variables, it is amazing children cope so well.

Don't neglect the fact that these powers of visual discrimination are drawn upon in non-letter settings, like jigsaws and matching games too. All the activities suggested for helping pre-reading, will be useful for writing too. You will tend to find that actually making the letters and building his own words, has a refining impact on your child's listening and reading abilities.

Observing sounds: Ear hear

To be able to start writing conventionally, your child must know the letter sounds and the names of the letters of the alphabet and have a sight vocabulary of a few key words, such as his name. Other key words are the sort that jump out of story books, such as 'dragon' and 'giant', or those around us such as 'on' and 'Sainsbury's'. There may be far fewer words which your child will feel confident enough to attempt to write compared to those he will try to read. This is because in order to write he has to pay more attention to fine detail to build up words, whereas when reading he focuses on getting meaning from the text as a whole.

Spoken language is broken down into units called phonemes. These are the smallest elements of sound which can change the meaning of a word. Think of the distinction between 'cat' and 'cap': the visual difference is perhaps greater than the variation in sound.

Games where you play with similar words train your child to hear the sound variations and to notice patterns in the image of the words. Later we look at the way schools apply these skills. For now just enjoy the excitement of finding rhymes to say and read together, and share stories which use this technique. Exploit the zany humour of making up your own nonsense poems with words offering similar sound patterns.

Practical tips for promoting pencil power

- Tracing, colouring, dot-to-dot and copying are all ways of improving pencil control. There are several entertaining sets available which lead from pencil play, patterning and tracing to instructions on lower case letter formation. These are fine as long as your child feels relaxed and confident, and if they offer sufficient revision to consolidate his skills.

- Adapt the approach to make the design of these pictures of more personal interest to your child.

- Offer felt pens and other special equipment as a means of livening up letter practice.

- Create interesting pictures using letter shapes. Mazes and tracing patterns which have a fun purpose such as matching or helping a lost creature reach home, are more likely to captivate than dry uninteresting pages with little visual appeal.

- Teach him to write his name by writing it and getting him to copy over using the correct strokes. Then offer faint dots and finally just a start position or a name card to copy. Use plain paper to start with but then progress to wide-lined sheets if he seems ready. Most of all, enjoy writing and feeling the shape of those personal letters in sand, flour, salt, using a paintbrush, chalk or playdough.

- Offer a variety of paper to early writers. The blank white page may offer space for large writing, but it gives no lines to guide your child's placing and orientation of letters.

- When you are asking her to concentrate on letter writing, make sure that she is sitting comfortably with good lighting and the paper at a suitable angle.

Everyone needs a personal signature!

Left or right: Getting the upper hand

Some toddlers show a strong preference for using one hand from a very early age, whilst others need to decide because they are starting school. If your child can use either hand, appears to be left-handed, or if his dominant eye is on the opposite side to his dominant foot or hand, you probably need to offer him greater support and more practice.

Left-handers are often helped by tilting the paper slightly clockwise and downwards. Give your child plenty of space to work using soft crayons and pencils and ensure his grip is correct and comfortable (see page 29). You should prevent him from using a crab-like position, hooking his hand over the top of his writing. This position will make it difficult for him to cope with writing tasks quickly and accurately. Left-handers will be discussed later in more detail (see page 82). For now, a stick to laying the correct foundations and to observing him carefully to confirm which is his dominant hand. Offer him lots of entertaining reasons for drawing and play patterning games which focus on getting him to look and scribble from left to right. His natural eye movement may be in the opposition direction so early training is essential.

Keeping it creative and maintaining confidence

In parallel with pencil-control tasks and games which concentrate on correct formation and spelling, do encourage play-writing. Children develop an early sense of right and wrong, of those who can write and those who can't. You want to avoid your child feeling a failure before he's even taken up the challenge of trying to write.

Show him the enjoyment attached to writing short letters and rhymes, and encourage him to try to produce writing alone. Explain that the main thing is that he can interpret what the writing says, and so can read it back to you. If he is still reluctant, suggest that he helps a baby brother or toy to write a letter.

Continue trying to create a need for writing in his imaginative play (see pages 25 and 67). This isn't easy, nor will you always know how to respond to the odd symbols he does produce. (I'll suggest some approaches when we look at emergent writing in schools on page 107).

Sean asked me to spell out signs for his grocery shop

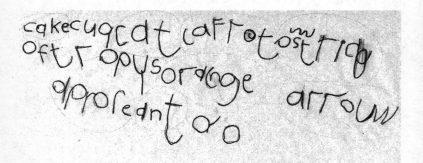

while Holly invented her own menu by copying from a book.

PART 1: FOUNDATIONS IN WRITING

This little girl is already confidently tracing over letters.

CHAPTER FOUR

Learning to read at school

Once you've survived the initial traumas of your child starting school, adjusting to a new routine and helping your child settle happily, you'll be looking for evidence of early reading progress. Teachers share your concerns and appreciate the power of literacy to liberate and extend their pupils. The emphasis on language skills takes many different forms, not all of which are automatically obvious.

Good communications with the school

One of the first jobs of the school is to inform you and to build up a sense that you are partners in your child's learning. Initiation periods for parent and child are quite common, with afternoon visits for 'junior' being matched by talks to explain things to you. Most primary heads deliberately work to achieve an approachable image, but they are busy and may rely on you to make the first move. Open access is fine as long as you are confident about getting involved and know how to go about it.

Your own image of schools and teachers can present a barrier to building up a strong relationship. Perhaps you have a vague school phobia, rather like the way I feel when I am sitting in a dentist's waiting room. At any rate, you probably won't have been inside a school for many years. The Lilliput scale of everything, including the chair you're invited to sit on, the strange little toilets and the constant flow of jostling uniformed bodies, is enough to unnerve anyone.

What you see may also jar with your personal memory of school. Gone are the rows of wooden desks, hushed children and a teacher sternly poised by the blackboard. Don't let the chatter of children working in groups put you off: there really is plenty of learning going on. Apart from the children themselves, look at the variety of work on display and the way it is treated by the teacher. Colourful, stimulating displays are a hallmark of most lively classrooms.

The class teacher will probably also surprise you with her approachable, down-to-earth manner. Not the austere creature you remember! It is in your child's interest that you work together to form a partnership to support your child's learning. To do this you must develop an appreciation for what goes on behind the school gates. Many children say remarkably little about their hours at school and any information has to be prized out of them. Don't feel left in the dark. Take leads offered by the school or individual teachers and get involved from the start. This doesn't mean you're being pushy or difficult; you are establishing vital links which will help ensure your continued, informed and positive involvement throughout your child's school career.

Getting a foothold

Your distance from the classroom will increase as your child grows more confident and independent in his new surroundings. At first you will probably be invited in to help him off with his coat, or you will at least be clearly evident at the school gate. Since children settle in to school in many different ways, most reception classes have a relaxed approachability, welcoming your 'intrusion'. As your child matures he will be far less happy to see you hovering around the class-room door. He may be embarrassed by your attention or could even equate your visits with the sense that something is wrong. Counter this by making the most of informal opportunities to chat from the start; your later involvement will then be quite natural.

A word of warning
Teachers are extremely busy. They have very little 'non-contact' time, without the constraints of looking after a class-load of children. Take the lead from them, by being sensitive to individual circumstances, and making genuine offers of help and support. Your child's teacher will value your expertise and interest. Schools increasingly look upon parental involvement as being of mutual benefit to teacher, parent and child. A posi-tive, friendly and welcoming atmosphere is the basic thing to look for, but you will need more specific information from the school if you are to be fully supportive at home.

A book in a bag: Home reading

Reading is the most common and obvious link with the language teaching that goes on in schools. It is also an important example of how your role as co-educator can be greatly improved through good communication. Most parents have the impression that any-thing that comes home from school must be read through by their child and then returned, but it is easy to get the wrong messages and to put unnecessary pressure on your child if you don't know the teacher's objectives. This is where meetings explaining the school's language policy, and perhaps a reading diary for teacher's and parents' comments, are invaluable.

Find out about the school's reading policy and materials

Perhaps the school relies on one or a number of 'core' reading schemes. (More about reading schemes on page 53). The language content and approach of schemes vary, and this affects the way they should be read with your child. There may also be a system of supplementary readers, library books and little books chosen freely by your child.

It is difficult for a parent wanting a sense of logical progression always to appreciate the flow of books in a bag. At this stage don't be too concerned if some books seem too easy as it will take a few weeks for your child's teacher to assess the individual level of each child. What you need to know is how each book is selected, whether it's one for you to read to your child, or whether he's expected to join in. A highly structured book with little story content will need to be handled differently to one with more natural story language and detail.

Enjoyment

The key principal for all reading activities with your child must be enjoyment and confidence building. To achieve this your child needs a wide variety of books to stimulate his interest and motivate him to learn to read independently. So whatever books come home, find a time when your child is relaxed and keen to join in. Don't attempt reading when he's yawning or tetchy after a hard day's concentration, or try to squeeze it in two minutes before his favourite television programme.

Enjoyment also means being patient when the same book turns up for the third night in a row. If he needs the comfort and security of the familiar, let him for a while. Progress will follow when he's ready, and when the teacher can tempt him onto something new. Refer back to all the foundation games on pages 9—11 and forward to suggestions on page 106, for entertaining ways of securing basic skills.

This parent aptly defines the golden rule:

❛ Making work fun is most important. Kathryn has gone from strength to strength.' ❜

How to share books with your child

Follow this guide as a way of using books from school that you are unfamiliar with.

- Find a suitable time and place. There should be plenty of warmth and cuddles with any reading activity. Although it isn't easy, make time so that you don't feel hurried. This will enable you to talk freely about the book and to give your child the feeling that you value this time together. I know that with toddlers clamouring for attention and older children demanding to know where their cub uniform is, you can't always create these conditions.

- Before you read the book, look at it together. Perhaps your child has already read it to his teacher, or he has chosen it himself. Give him the confidence of being the expert, of knowing the joke on the last page or of having inside knowledge about the characters. This encourages him to talk about the book, focus on the text and predict the storyline. If neither of you is familiar with the book, flip through the pages together using the pictures to guess about the content.

- Unless your child wants to read alone, start from the cover, reading the book carefully to him. Pause to discuss ideas and interests, developing information given by the pictures and predicting outcomes.

- Match this by focusing on the text, pointing to each word as you read it (being careful not to block his vision). Discuss key words, as well as those which start with the same sound or which have similar endings.

- Use discretion with this approach. You may want to read the story straight through first to get the maximum enjoyment from it. Constant checks can lose the flow or irritate your listener.

- Suggest that you read the book through together, paus-

PART 2: LEARNING TO READ AT SCHOOL

ing to let your child fill in endings or key words, particularly those which can be prompted by looking at the pictures. Praise any efforts he makes.

- Don't correct mistakes he makes if the word he uses retains the sense of the passage. You can later re-read and point out the actual word, perhaps focusing on the initial letter to help.

- If your child is keen, ask him then to read the book on his own. Give him plenty of time to guess at new words, to re-read and to correct his own mistakes. Familiarity with the book should boost his confidence to try reading alone.

- When he gets stuck, point to clues which may be useful. This could be the picture, or the whole word, the sound it starts with or the flow of what's gone before. It's often handy to re-read up to that point, and to read to the end of the sentence before trying to fit in an appropriate word. All children are different. If your child appears anxious or annoyed at his difficulty, give him the word he needs with the minimum of fuss.

- Keep your child interested and enthusiastic. Use whatever approaches work for him. Talk all the time as you're sharing books. This helps him learn ways of tackling new words and, of course, should increase his pleasure and understanding of what he's reading. Praise all his efforts and help him build upon a sense of success.

Reading at home spills out all the warmth, adventure and sheer fun of books. Later in your child's schooling, you may be encouraged to try different styles of shared reading. Whatever method you use, if your child is not happy or feels under pressure, explain his response to his teacher and work out a different approach.

Reading in class

❝ *We didn't read in class today!* ❞

Don't worry if you hear this refrain fairly frequently, especially if you are regularly getting books from school. What your child classifies as 'reading' may be confined to those brief snatches of individual reading time with his teacher, possibly with what he sees as his 'proper' reading book. Of course these times are crucial for assessing your child's specific needs and for teaching him methods of tackling new words just when he needs them. But the teacher has limited time to devote to this intensive form of reading. She may opt for less frequent but longer sessions to promote enjoyment and facilitate understanding. In his earliest phase, she will want to make shared reading times as frequent as possible, but will supplement them with many other approaches to help develop reading skills.

- Teachers build upon the knowledge each individual child brings to school. This will, of course, require careful observation and assessment, so that the teacher can draw your child on from the stage he has reached. His teacher will note his responses in all of the activities outlined below, and tailor the reading programme to suit his needs.

- Reading around the classroom. A lively classroom has many notices and sources of written information to enjoy. This starts with your child being able to identify his peg, books and work tray. He will also quickly learn how to return the puzzles, construction toys and paints to the rightly labelled shelf. There will also be notice boards and interest displays, probably with captions and questions to stimulate your child's interest.

- Books! Your child's class should be alive with interestingly displayed books. In addition, there will be samples of the children's own writing on display and poetry books and story tapes to enjoy. There will be opportunities for your child to dip in to these books, sometimes with the teacher's assistance.

- Language games. Part of the day will probably be spent talking as a class, sharing ideas and drawing out your child's awareness of sounds, letters and words through games and wordplay. Later he will learn to work in groups, playing games which develop his language skills.

- Group reading sessions. The teacher will create frequent opportunities to read to her class. This includes traditional story sessions, looking closely at specific books to illustrate a point, sharing books from the reading scheme and 'big book' sessions. The latter are a lovely way of getting everyone involved. Many schemes produce these giant texts in parallel with smaller books, so your child can enjoy learning in a group and then can follow it up with individual reading later.

- Your child's teacher will exploit the links between reading and writing so that the writing activities are also learning opportunities for reading.

- The class may also have a 'silent' reading time each day. This allows everyone, including the teacher, to choose a book and settle quietly to explore it, either alone or quietly with a friend. Your child will then be able to sample some of the books which have caught his interest and he will see everyone else valuing the same experience.

- The National Curriculum endorses the importance of children having a variety of reading experiences. Children learn different reading strategies because the teacher encourages breadth and variety, tailoring methods to suit each child. Your child reads because he needs and wants to make sense of the words.

What makes a good school reading programme?
Here are some things to think about when you are deciding
upon a choice of school, or to find out through contact with
your child's teachers if she has already started.

A school reading programme should:

- offer breadth and flexibility;
- be well planned, so that the Head and your child's
  class teacher clearly understand where they are aiming;
- contains books which are matched carefully to your
  child's ability, so that his efforts to read are successful;
- take a balanced approach so that your child has time
  for individual, group and 'whole class' sessions;
- use time effectively, so that the teacher's intensive
  sessions with just your child are created at times when
  both are able to concentrate;
- be alive with creative ideas, energy and enthusiasm so
  that this positive appeal is passed on to the children.

Learning should be fun. Reading and writing are hard work, but if
your child appreciates the rewards he will be keen to join in.

Reading methods explained

Before we leave the reception class enjoying their reading, I must
offer a few words of explanation regarding the Reading Debate
which has had so much media coverage. There have been a number
of reports which have suggested that there has been a decline in
reading standards during the past decade. They have been used to
support a 'Back to Basics' campaign, and to attack the use of 'real
books' (i.e. books that aren't part of a scheme) in the teaching of
reading.

Firstly, I would suggest that a good teacher will succeed in helping your child learn to read whatever the method. Secondly, and

more importantly, most teachers have always employed a variety of methods to tie in with individual needs and to provide different kinds of learning opportunities. What really rings true through all the confusing debate is the need to offer a range of methods and to be sensitive to the way different children approach reading.

Are reading standards in decline?

Evidence about declining standards is largely inconclusive and can't be considered without looking at how these standards are measured. One of the objectives of the new Standard Tests is to provide useful data to help with this assessment, and to streamline teaching more efficiently to focus on areas of need. But the class teacher's profile of each pupil is crucial too, as only this can help you appreciate how your child is doing. This is your main concern, rather than what level your child has reached in the Standard Tests, and what assessment process was used.

A small-scale Ofsted survey conducted in 1993 found reading standards to be satisfactory or better in 90 per cent of Reception and 85 per cent of Year 1 classes. Background and pre-school experience had a strong influence on pupil's performance. Encouraging reports may not be widely publicised. While there is still cause for concern, the positive effects of reading at home remain our priority.

If we do accept that there has been a decline in standards, there are other potential culprits apart from those 'real books'. The 1990 HMI Report showed that most schools use a variety of methods. Schools which stuck rigidly to only one approach were likely to have less satisfactory standards of reading. So what else could be affecting reading standards?

The additional strain on teaching time caused by the National Curriculum has led to a reduction in potential reading development time. Recent changes in the breadth and assessment of the Curriculum have tried to address these problems.

Reading standards also reflect wider social concerns such as changes in library provision, the cost and availability of good books, and how we as adults value reading.

The main methods of teaching your child to read

Here is a checklist of methods used in schools. Remember that a mixed diet is the best provision for most children. It is up to the skill of your child's teacher to match the approach to your child's specific needs. Obviously the school's policy and emphasis will be reflected in its reading resources. But budgets are tight and there must be practical limits to the range of reading books offered in schools.

When many of us learnt to read there was a strong emphasis on decoding, of using whole words or letter-sounds in isolation to work out the meaning. Two methods reflect this emphasis:

Phonics

Perhaps the most sensitive word in the Reading Debate! This approach focuses on your child being taught letter sounds, blends and clusters to help 'word attack' skills for reading. This requires reading to be taught in a highly structured way. Your child starts by learning the sounds of individual letters, but there are 44 separate sounds to distinguish in all. A working knowledge of the alphabet is a must, as in an ability to distinguish the starting sounds in words. Once your child is familiar with the most common sounds made by individual letters, he will learn 'blends' such as 'br' and 'sl' where two sounds are pushed together. The next stage will include 'clusters' of letters which make one sound, such as 'str' and 'spr', together with 'digraphs' such as 'th', 'sh' and 'ch'. This last group illustrates the complexity of phonics as the new sounds are not linked to the two letter sounds involved.

Phonics requires a highly structured reading scheme so that children meet familiar sounds to de-code. This makes it very difficult to offer lively or interesting books in the early stages. The language is forced and unnatural, so your child tends to neglect the meaning of the text.

Apart from this, there are very real complications in trying to apply a logic to, for example, the 'y' sound in 'my', 'eye', 'buy', 'pie' and 'high'. Irregularities need to be learnt. This method requires the teacher to use great imagination and energy to make the learning of sounds fun and relevant. It usually involves many matching, posting and guessing games linking similar sounds or pictures of objects to their corresponding initial sounds.

Your child needs to distinguish tiny changes in sounds for this method to work. Those children who suffer frequent problems with colds or who have weaker auditory skills will therefore be at a disadvantage.

This is not to say that phonic skills don't have an important place in reading development, merely that they are very limiting if used to the exclusion of other methods and more natural books.

Look and say method

This method also relies on a carefully controlled reading scheme, as children learn to distinguish whole words in isolation. Your child will build up a sight vocabulary of common words, many of which are difficult to guess at using other methods. The teacher may use flashcards or games, perhaps sending words home to learn. Once your child remembers some words, he will be given books containing the same vocabulary.

Like phonics, the drawback of this approach is that children are introduced to stilted and artificial vocabulary. They are not given strategies to tackle new words, and they neglect the meaning of what they are reading. If your child has a poor visual memory or problems with his sight, his progress will be slow.

There are benefits to this approach, particularly with children who have a good visual memory. As well as needing a bank of phonic knowledge, a fluent reader needs to have a large sight vocabulary, and this approach sharpens his skill. If your child uses

Look and say in conjunction with other methods, he will be able to learn by whatever approach best fits his needs.

Language experience approach

Leading on from Look and say, teachers often relate a child's reading to what he wants to say in his writing. This extends the emphasis so that the teaching of key words takes place in a whole sentence which has a direct personal meaning for your child. The idea is to build upon your child's knowledge of language so that he can predict words. He will enjoy re-reading his own creations, but as his ideas and self-expression become more complex, so the approach becomes rather unmanageable. (See pages 63–64 for further details.)

Apprenticeship approach

This is usually referred to as the 'real books' method, because of the importance attached to offering your child a wide range of quality reading books from the start. All that we mean by 'real books', is those which are not linked to any specially devised scheme. In fact, there are several ways that 'real books' are classified to provide a structure from which your child can choose appropriate books.

This method is often seen as being extreme, and to be in direct conflict with the traditional wisdom of phonics. Good teachers will use both methods to compliment each other and to offer your child different ways of tackling new words.

Where Apprenticeship is different is in its emphasis on first giving your child confidence in reading. Your child will act like a reader before he truly is one, but in doing so he is learning vital strategies to help him take off towards independent reading. He will be offered a wide selection of books to choose from, which draw upon his interests and his knowledge of story language. As he is more actively involved, his motivation should be stronger.

The teacher will share a book with your child and follow the sort of strategies I discussed earlier, so that he increasingly pays more attention to the words and uses the context to guess at new words. My experience has been that the early stages of this approach can seem slow and confusing, but with careful planning and control by the teacher your child will learn to read with confidence, understanding and enjoyment. However, there are children who need a more structured and limited introduction to reading and the teacher must be sensitive to this.

Very few schools use this approach alone. Those schools which use 'real books' extensively attract and train a staff who are confident in how to structure and assess your child's reading development. Media crisis stories have tended to neglect the merits of this approach. It is certainly not a soft option and relies strongly on meticulous planning and monitoring by committed teachers. Don't forget that there will be many other reading strategies applied to help your child discover the joys of reading.

A word about reading schemes

Many schools rely to a greater or lesser extent upon reading schemes. They will usually have a core reader which is used most extensively throughout the lower school. This helps provide a clear developmental structure and it fits our own memories of how we learnt to read. However, most schools recognise the limitations of following just one scheme, so they supplement their main choice with other materials. The accurate assessment and matching of different levels for each scheme is difficult to achieve though.

The National Curriculum endorses the importance of providing a good range of books for early readers. Although modern reading schemes look more lively, some still suffer from the cardboard language that you and I might have experienced:

'See John, see the little dog run! Look, John, look!'

Yes, I did make the line up, but it's not unusual to find similar stilted language in children's early readers. Apart from being boring, this type of text doesn't let your child apply his wider knowledge to the text as there is often precious little context to interpret.

Some of the most common reading schemes found in schools include:

- *One Two Three and Away* (HarperCollins), which supports Look and say methods;
- Ladybird schemes are often used as supplementary readers; there are several different schemes;
- *New Way*, which supports Phonic methods;
- *Ginn 360*, long-standing and recently updated scheme which uses a combination of methods, including Phonics and Look and say. This is achieved through a structured approach with a gradual build-up of core vocabulary.

Several more recent schemes counter the risks of boredom through using a strong storyline, children's humour and more natural language to maintain interest. There is also far greater effort to use bold, attractive illustrations. Some of the books your child brings home to share with you have a stronger entertainment value than others. Aim to draw out the enjoyment of the book, perhaps spending less time on one which offers your child no interest. Mention it to his teacher if this is regularly the case, and try to use other approaches to maintain his interest in reading.

Recent schemes give a more rounded language experience, with the welcome inclusion of rhymes, poetry and non-fiction material. Newer schemes which you might encounter include:

- the *Longman Reading World*;
- the *Oxford Reading Tree*;
- *Sunshine Books*;
- *Storychest*;
- *Bookshelf*;
- *Book Bus*;
- *All Aboard*.

Many reading schemes offer the teacher additional material, such as large books to share with groups or the whole class, tapes,

PART 2: LEARNING TO READ AT SCHOOL

worksheets and even computer games. These can all supplement your child's reading experience in the classroom.

Whatever schemes your child's school uses, keep two things in mind:

1 Don't get stuck in the 'on to the next book' rut. The real horror of schemes is that they emphasise a ladder of progression, so it's easy to want your child to be striving for the next level book. I know it's impossible not to notice if his friends are all taking home a 'more advanced' book, or if you're given the same book to re-read again and again. Remember that learning to read is not a race, and that the main purpose of being involved is to aid your child's confidence and enthusiasm. You can't hope to do this if you're feeling the pressure to move on, rather than enjoying what your child can do.

2 Reading schemes, even the best ones, are just one type of book to which your child should have access. Concentrate on offering different books at home and sharing as many styles as interest your child, giving ample time to enjoy the beauty and richness of picture books.

CHAPTER FIVE

How your child learns to write in a reception class

It will be harder for you to assess what's going on with your child's writing development than with her reading, mainly because nothing comes home regularly. It will help if you take steps to find out about the school's policy, ask questions and respond to invitations to visit the classroom.

Teachers are sensitive to your desire to find out what your child has been doing, so they will usually create displays or leave messages inviting you to look at your child's work. Perhaps there is an end-of-the-week policy, where every child's best work is open for admiration. Do make a point of looking at this work with your child, so that you can praise her efforts and discuss what she's done. Ask her to explain things and show you special features of her work. She'll love the satisfaction of her labour being valued and of her own judgement being taken seriously.

Why should I write?

We have already looked at the complexity involved in the physical act of writing. I was reminded, when flicking through my Thesaurus for inspiration, of all the other 'hard work' labels you could apply to the task of writing. Yes, it can be a 'drudge', a 'grind' and a 'slog' because it is messy, time-consuming and difficult. On the other hand, it is a unique means of self-expression and a source of great satisfaction when we get it right.

If we're honest, when faced with something difficult, such as reversing into a tight parking space, it's far simpler not to try. What you have to do is find ways of showing your child the value of writing, giving it a purpose and a pleasure which draws her on to discover more about it. This is exactly what teachers try to do at school, but they have many more individual interests to satisfy and a tight checklist of teaching objectives to meet.

Like most young writers, Ben's message is proudly egocentric!

Assessing what your child already knows

What's in a name?

Like reading, the teacher will begin by discovering what each of her charges knows about writing. Many children will be able to identify and write the letters in their own name, so they will have chances to write out decorative labels and enjoy their own competence. All the while, the teacher will be looking at how the children are forming their letters, what grip they use, their levels of concentration and control. Remember, this will be different for every child, so there is a fair bit of observation required! The teacher will also discuss letter shapes and sounds and will begin to build a picture of each child's phonological awareness.

All these little learners want to write their names.

Free writing

Your child should be encouraged to have sessions of free writing (or 'emergent writing') right from the start of his school career. Ideally this will flow naturally from the energetic scribble he has offered you at home. If you have always admired these efforts and valued them as the first real signs of wanting to write, then your child is likely to have a positive attitude to recording his ideas on paper. I will discuss the value of 'emergent writing' in more detail later, but please don't be put off by the confusing squiggles with which you're confronted. These provide everyone with vital information about what children actually know about and can apply to writing. This includes any real letter shapes used, whether there is a logical flow across the page from left to right, and whether there are clear spaces between the 'words'. Later your child's teacher will use free writing to assess how much your child appreciates about spelling and punctuation. The ideas which prompted your child's writing are of prime importance, and it is these which should be focused upon and discussed.

Knowing the letters

Your child's teachers will also want to spend time finding out what he knows about the alphabet and letter sounds. She will play alphabet games and use rhymes, songs and humour to draw out his sensitivity to letters and sounds. This is separate to the mechanical skill of teaching handwriting. However, there is now evidence to suggest that the skills overlap, so that the pattern of letters, and the flow of our handwriting, have benefits in helping with spelling and reading.

All teachers are required to keep a portfolio of children's work,

Allow plenty of time to explore letters and words.

with dated samples of their writing for you to discuss together. This is a perfect way of being able to analyse your child's progress, and of highlighting areas where she might need more help.

What writing activities are going on in the classroom?

There is a great deal of variety in the types of writing activities your child will experience. The 'proper writing' you remember from your own school days is only part of a total diet. The teacher will want to ensure that she is using different approaches when there are different objectives. For example, when she wants to encourage your child's creative energies, she may write down some of his ideas for him, but when she wants to develop his hand control she may give him three words to copy.

Some common writing methods

Talking and writing

Many writing activities are prompted through class or group discussion, so there is a great deal of positive language buzzing around which you never see. In the early stages this is often a 'whole class' session, with the teacher writing down key words and ideas which arise out of the discussion. This could have a creative purpose, for example re-telling and elaborating upon a favourite story. It could be that the class is looking closely at an object or trying to record a simple sequence of events accurately. There are also many opportunities for sharing the fun of rhymes, for writing down words which have something in common or for listing words beginning with the same initial letter sound.

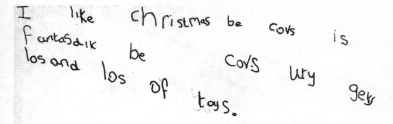

I like christmas be covs is fantasdik be covs los and los of toys.

I liked the bit where they were on the magic mat.

8.12

To Seah.

Merry Christmas
Love
Jennifer   xx

Everyone loves writing about Christmas!

Drawing and writing

Your child expresses her ideas through her drawings, which may become beautifully elaborate and inventive. The teacher may develop this by writing captions in response to pictures, or by inviting your child to write a short response.

HELP YOUR CHILD WITH READING AND WRITING

Jennifer's accomplished writing makes you want to sail away!

Group writing

As your child's social confidence grows, so it's more likely that the teacher will use group sessions as a means of pooling ideas or writing simple messages for a real audience. This could mean that your child helps develop a story sequence with other children, perhaps with an adult helping them record their ideas. There will also be chances to write simple letters and messages to other children in the class or school. Perhaps the children write messages to the teacher, reminding her of books they'd like to read or songs they want to learn. These simple activities help give a positive meaning to your child's writing.

Copy writing: More about me!

There will be regular chances for personal writing, whether this is reporting about what your child did over the weekend, responding to a story or listing favourite food. Your child may begin by drawing a picture and then, after a discussion, the teacher writes a sentence underneath. Before your child is able to form the letters independently, he may be asked to trace over the teacher's writing. This helps reinforce ideas about letter sizing and spacing, and is a useful aid to reading as he will then re-read his caption with the teacher.

Once the teacher is confident that your child can form his letters correctly, she will encourage him to copy out the words directly underneath her own writing. He is still being helped with spacing and is being offered the correct spellings and punctuation to copy.

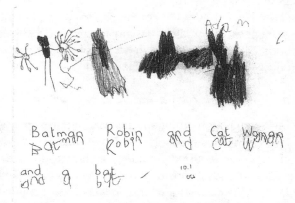

Adam first dictates then copies writing about his favourite characters.

Copy writing can also mean literally words that are copied from a blackboard or a piece of paper. The problem from the parent's perspective is to discover where the words came from. What looks lovely may not have actively involved your child in creative writing. This type of exercise has its merits, but it is only one aspect of learning to be a writer.

Breakthrough

This is the word linked to the 'Breakthrough to Literacy' material which became widely available in schools during the 1970s in response to the Language experience approach to reading. Basically, your child has a folder holding over a hundred of the words most commonly used by children, as a basis for helping him to write independently. It is a tricky process though. First, he has to have the idea of what he wants to write. Then he has to find each word, remove it from his folder and stick it on a stand. If he's using any more original words, he'll have to ask the teacher to write them out on specially-sized card so they can join the others on his stand. Finally, he'll have to copy the sentence carefully into his book. What you see is one brief sentence: you don't know the extent of the process that got the words there in the first place. Because the words are fiddly and children tire of the process as they create more complex sentences, the material is no longer widely used. Like most methods it has merits, and can be a useful confidence bridge for children just starting to write independently.

Wordbanks, dictionaries and independent spelling

Early writing is amazingly tiring and demanding. This includes the physical task of making recognisable letters and words, and the mental concentration required in finding out how to spell the words you want to say. It's not surprising that teachers try to ease the load.

It may be that the class as a whole collects lists of useful words, or that the teacher makes a special display or box full of words so that your child can find his spelling independently. Ultimately though, she becomes something of a walking dictionary, distributing spelling at a frightening rate. It's one of the delights of teaching, that you may be asked to spell 'yesterday' one minute and 'gladiator' the next!

Encouraging children to write freely reduces the dictionary role, but requires careful interpretation and analysis with the 'author'. (See page 107 for details of emergent writing.)

Alphabet fun

Whatever methods you use to teach reading and writing, the alphabet sounds and letter shapes need to be learnt as quickly as possible. This will be reflected in some of the work you see in a reception class. It could be that the children create their own illustrated alphabet books, perhaps on an animals or a seasonal theme. There may

santa laid the presents
under the tree

Thursday 6th January

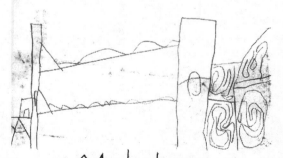

My bedroom
In the corner of My bed room there is a
chair it can change In to a bed
bdom.

Getting any words written is a challenge for many, but enjoy what your child can accomplish and share his sense of achievement.

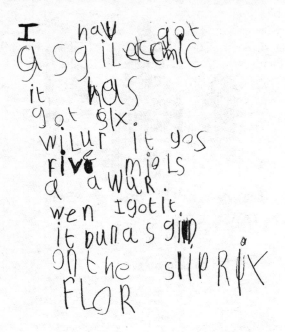

This reads: I have got a Scalextric (and) it has got six wheels it goes five miles a hour. When I got it it done a skid on the slippery floor.

be worksheets related to television programmes or to the reading scheme, with an emphasis on simple phonic rules.

Letterland material is very popular in schools, providing child-friendly characterisations of each letter to aid phonic awareness and letter formation. (See the Appendix on page 220 for details of material available to parents.) Your child may be more likely to visualise 'h' because she remembers stories about hairy hat-man, and can recall the starting sound easily.

We look at different styles of handwriting on pages 78–84, as part of a wider focus on presentation skills.

Writing through play

Just as you encouraged your child to write when creating a clinic or lunar module at home, so there should be plenty of chances for 'play-writing' at school. Often the whole classroom will be swamped by a particular idea, the walls and home corner being taken over to tie in with a particular interest or project. So a space theme could prompt anything from instructions on how to brush your teeth with a weightless toothbrush, to the drama of landing a lunar module or letters to family left on Earth. Unfortunately, a busy classroom cannot always cater for spontaneous individual ideas for writing. This is something you are better placed to do at home.

Where do I fit in?

With reading, you probably feel on quite a sure footing if your child's school is regularly sending home books for you to share. It's far harder to be confident that you are complementing the writing activities going on in school. Continue with entertaining efforts to help hand control and letter formation. Some form of presentation work is useful throughout the primary years, particularly if you create reasons why the writing should be neat and correct. Drawing, dot-to-dot, mazes, crazy colouring and tracing will certainly not harm your child's progress either. Some children are keener to write and draw at home after they've started school, while others need coaxing. This often means choosing the right moment, being actively involved yourself and keeping the sessions short but successful.

What about the creative side of writing?

Ask your child's teacher to suggest starting points for writing. Your

> **A checklist for making writing special**
> - Create a cosy place with space, surfaces and chairs which match your child's needs.
> - Give him your time and support, praising his efforts and working in collaboration.
> - Collect interesting objects, comics, pictures and books which might stimulate your writing sessions together.
> - Look for practical ways to get him writing, such as writing messages and menu requests when friends visit, or sending off for details of the Thunderbird Fan Club.
> - Provide interesting material for writing such as new pens, special paper and trimmings for decorating home-made books. (See page 25 for details about how to create an interesting variety of books together.)
> - Notice his special tastes and current fads, then find ways of writing about them.
> - Play games which need you to record answers or ideas.
> - Give your child special responsibility for writing replies to invitations and recording his important events in the family diary.
> - Praise and talk through all his efforts and encourage friends and family to do the same.

child's favourite television characters may spark off ideas, much as they do for his imaginative play. Tap his inventive energy, thinking up ways to solve mysterious problems, new versions of favourite tales

and captions to go under old comic strips. Books and cards
of interesting sizes and shapes, a new set of fine felts or some
gummed paper shapes, can all provoke curiosity and a willingness
to try writing together. The one essential ingredient for most beginners is your time, support and praise.

Something special

How do you let your child feel in control of his writing, when he
lacks so many of the fundamental skills? The answer seems to lie
in accepting a compromise and in trying to excite him about what
he's doing, so that he gains confidence and satisfaction by completing work well. Your support should be subtle and sensitive, so he
responds to your suggestions, but still feels the ideas are his own.

CHAPTER SIX

Foundations in spelling and handwriting

After reading, spelling and handwriting seems to cause most anxiety to parents. There are three main reasons for this:

1 We have fears prompted by debates about standards and concern about children leaving schools with a level of English which doesn't satisfy work requirements.

> ❝ It is no good having great ideas if you can't write them clearly for people to read. ❞

> ❝ I want my child to learn good English, so that he knows how to write properly. ❞

> ❝ They take marks off if you can't spell when it gets to GCSE exams, so it's important he learns his spellings now. ❞

2 Learning spellings, taking home lists and handwriting practice are real memories of our own past. It's therefore quite natural that we should expect to offer similar support to our own children.

3 These skills are visible, we feel we can easily get involved because we know what to look for. Besides, they are both easy to do at home, especially with so many study books now on

the market. Many schools support parents in this by offering spelling lists or work to copy out at home. This provides a reassuring basis for your involvement.

Only one way to teach spelling?

Perhaps you see learning spellings as a safe bet. You can't confuse your child if there's only one right answer. Unfortunately, nothing in language development is learnt in isolation. Like every other part of learning to read and write, there is more than one approach to teaching spellings. This is not to say that there is only one right method, nor that efforts to help your child learn spelling rules have no value. Provided she feels positive and enjoys the process, you will be aiding her memory and study skills even if she forgets some of her spellings.

Recent research has pointed to the importance of learning spellings in a meaningful way. As you read with your child, chances to show him rules and patterns in words will occur naturally. He'll appreciate the reason because he wants to make sense of the story. In the same way, if you encourage him to try and spell independently from an early stage, the mistakes he makes will show you areas where he needs help.

Proof-reading allows you to pinpoint words he finds particularly difficult. Start by drawing his attention to the word and see if he can write down alternative spellings. This offers an important visual clue to help him remember. Reinforce this by pointing out the same word, or ones which follow the same pattern, when you read together. In this way your child learns words when he needs them.

Trained teachers will be able to cope with your child's seemingly bizarre spellings. This is because invented spelling actually follows a pattern. We have to learn what help to offer and when.

What's wrong with spelling lists?

Few would deny that certain spelling rules and regularities should be learnt, or that it is vital that your child develops both a sight vocabulary and a strong bank of common words that he can spell instantly. But will your child learn most efficiently by being given lists of words? This depends upon your child's type of memory, and upon her teacher's ability to make connections and so help her both to remember and to apply her spelling skills when she needs them.

Spelling tests can cause stress. Handled badly, they can subject your child to feelings of humiliation and failure. I can remember a 'game' played at our school. The teacher hurled quickfire spellings at us, and only a correct answer ensured you could then go out to play. This may seem harmless enough, but it made that year at school a misery for me.

Your child needs to see spellings as a positive challenge, rather than something to be dreaded. Test tension isn't conducive to the accepting atmosphere which will encourage your child to experiment, take risks and learn through her mistakes.

For both reading and writing there are a small number of 'high frequency' words which your child will need to learn such as 'of', 'was' and 'that'. In fact a mere dozen or so words account for about a quarter of the total words your child will encounter in her reading. While this seems to support the use of spelling lists and a Look and say approach to reading, we must remember that your child also needs strategies to cope with attempting spellings for all the other words she reads far less frequently. Phonic skills and a detailed awareness of regular word patterns will help her achieve this goal. The words she learns should be visible to aid her memory and should fit in with a general framework of language. Chanting out the spellings of problem words rarely helps 'problem' spellers overcome their difficulties.

If your child enjoys spelling tests that's great, as memory plays a big part in being a competent speller. Find another route for those who find rote learning particularly unsuccessful.

If spelling tests don't work, how can I help?

Short, challenging quickfire tests still have a place in the spelling jungle, but the words they test must be related to your child's needs. The test is only for herself and should not be a means of comparison with others. There are many productive activities you can enjoy together working towards the same goal.

Sowing the seeds

From the moment she shows a real interest, draw your child's attention to words, the shape and corresponding sound patterns.

Use rhymes and jokes, tongue-twisters and songs to show links between words. For example, you could collect as many words as possible ending in '-at', then try creating nonsense verse with them.

As you share books together, point out the same patterns. Play 'word spot' games, hunting down the same word in different contexts. Try making deliberate mistakes by substituting similar words and seeing if you're detected.

Help, in all the ways suggested earlier, to foster phonic skills and to give your child a firm grounding in letter sounds and alphabet skills.

How do children learn to spell?

There is now a joint emphasis on both visual and aural memory. Spelling isn't just about building up sounds, it's also 'seeing' the total shape of a word. We need to offer activities which develop both these skills.

Once your child can read a little independently and writes confidently, here is one approach you could take:

1   Read through a piece of her writing together. Once you have discussed the ideas and praised her efforts, make a note of a couple of words she has spelt incorrectly.

2 Later draw her attention to these spellings. Ask her to re-read her work, and see if she reads the words correctly.

3 Look closely at the words together, and ask her to try an alternative spelling. Praise her efforts.

4 Give her the correct spelling. Ask her to copy it out, saying the word as she does so.

5 Try the Look, Cover, Write and Say, then Check technique:

> **Look** closely at the correct spelling, perhaps tracing over the letters and repeating the sounds.
>
> **Cover** the word up.
>
> **Write** the word from memory, **say**ing the sound or whole word as you do so.
>
> **Check** to see if you are correct. If you made a mistake, note where you went wrong and try again.

6 Don't let your child feel a failure. She needs to be relaxed and confident and to accept that making mistakes is an important part of learning and of finding out where we need most help.

Activities to help your child's spelling

Encourage your child to relate the spelling of a word to its meaning, to a funny image or known patterns, so that he feels confident about tackling the word next time.

Get your child into positive habits

- Ask her to leave a gap, line or symbol when she encounters a word she can't spell as this frees her to concentrate on what she's writing. Once she's finished she can proof-read her work.
- Use a spell-check on the computer.
- Try to spell independently by using a dictionary, picture clues, words from reference books, etc.
- Use the Look, Cover, Write and Say, then Check method outlined above.

    Encourage a sense of pride in the special writing she does

for other people. Remember a first draft is just that, and a diary note may be for her eyes only. However, a record review for her pen friend in Leeds should be spot on.

- A fast, flowing handwriting style helps spelling patterns. Practising strings of letters which occur regularly, such as '-tion', in a game will improve her speed and sizing of letters.

Fun and games with spellings

- Look for family games from Countdown, Scrabble and Boggle, to Hangman and 'I spell-spy' as a means of airing those spelling skills.
- Look for entertaining crossword and puzzle books which appeal to your child's current interests. Have a go at making up your own teasers, such as grids or pyramids of words which have a common core:

    air, pain, train, dainty, rainfall, fountain, etc.

- Play dictionary games, having taught your child how to work her way around one.
- Learn opposites and plurals, trying to use humour or word association to make them stick.
- Draw silly cartoons of prefixes, such as head -teacher, -ache, -first, -line, etc. Do the same for words such as 'car-pet', 'book-worm', and 'sub-marine', which have two distinct parts.
- Older children may find learning relevant spelling rules useful, but stick to the ones which have few exceptions to complicate matters. For example, 'i before e except after c when the i.e. rhymes with me' is an easy jingle to remember. Using a silly sentence like 'Oh the weird ways words deceive. See if you can conceive a way to seize these words and receive the right spelling', fixes the details further.
- Whilst many children find some rules fun, especially if taught like a sort of code, for others it is extremely hard to translate them to their general writing. Be sensitive to your own child's

needs. If quoting rules seems to depress or confuse her, try to link words visually or use a different approach.

Handwriting is hard work

You must have friends whose letters engage the whole family in a deciphering game. Strangely enough we tend to ignore such quirks as we get older, claiming that unusual lettering is distinctive, even a sign of maturity and character. Some writing is beautiful and has style and grace, but more importantly, it must be legible.

Whatever method and style your child's school uses, the task is to have her writing quickly, confidently and legibly as soon as possible. Contrast the rapid flow of her free-writing with the process of learning correct spelling and lettering. Then you'll appreciate why we want these skills established rapidly and effectively.

The National Curriculum requires children to have begun to write with 'clear, legible joined up writing' by Level 3. Children in primary schools have traditionally first learnt to print letters and have then gradually acquired a joined-up style or 'cursive' writing during their junior school years. Teachers don't want to feel that handwriting difficulties are holding back pupils who would otherwise have achieved Level 3. This has perhaps prompted greater thought about handwriting, with some questioning the wisdom of children effectively having to learn two different systems. Some schools now teach cursive writing from the start.

If you went into a French nursery, you'd be surprised to find the toddlers reading and writing script with joined up lettering. In this country, it was felt that clear printing aided correct letter formation and your child's ability to recognise letters. Yet before school, toddlers 'read' letters in many different guises. Real life words all around us offer a confusing variety of forms. If you show your child that there are several ways of writing the letter 'a', she will accept this diversity from the start. The argument against this is that it creates unnecessary confusion before skills and understanding are established.

Logical lettering: Learning how to write letters

This task may be very demanding for your child, particularly if she hasn't chosen to produce detailed drawings or play pencil games much in the past. Start by ensuring she gets her grip right, and encourage her to sit in a relaxed but sensible position, perhaps with the paper tilted slightly so she can see what she's doing. Make sure she has a soft, firm lead pencil and a triangular grip if extra control is useful. When your child starts to write letters there are a number of things she has to master:

- the 'start position' for each individual letter;
- the direction that she moves her pencil to form the letter shape;
- the relative size of the shapes she makes;
- the orientation of the letter. For example, 'b', 'd', 'p' and 'q' are similar shapes which have to be put in the right space to make sense;
- the space that she needs to leave between words so that her writing can be understood;
- she has to copy or remember the distinctive form which makes each particular letter. As she writes independently, she has to relate the visual memory of these squiggles to her mental memory of the sounds they make.

Phew! All this and you haven't begun to tackle what she wants to say, and how she's going to organise her ideas. It's no wonder that writing for beginners is hard work. We tend to forget this, partly because these skills should become second nature, but also because many of us only use writing regularly for scribbled memos, lists and letters.

Write or wrong?

Each school will decide its own handwriting policy, so check what guidelines your child's school offers parents. If you lack clear information try this lettering, which is used in many schools (see page 79).

Pay particular attention to the start positions and when you are required to take the pencil off the page. There are too many variations in style to cover, but look at the contrasting lettering of 'Reading and writing for pleasure' for some clues. Sources of advice are mentioned in the Appendix on page 212.

If you can, try to balance letter practice with games and patterns which encourage the same flow of shapes and with chances for your child to continue her free writing or scribble. Whatever she does, your praise will give her confidence to develop her skills further.

Match your expectations regarding her handwriting to what she is doing. If she's deep in creative thought her writing will not be as careful as when she's copying out her favourite poem or writing up a final draft of her letter to Gran.

Short, frequent sessions when you go over one or two letters or strings of letters, may be more successful than trying for all-round perfection too often.

Give your child the chance to evaluate her own strengths and difficulties and to share a sense of pride in how much she can do.

How is handwriting taught at school?

The first priority is to understand the style and process which the school uses. This may be:

- traditional print style lettering, usually starting with lower case letters before going on to capital letters;

PART 2: FOUNDATIONS IN SPELLING AND HANDWRITING

An example of standard lettering. Take care with start positions and the direction of the strokes. Using a thick pencil, encourage your child to copy these letters of the alphabet – or your tracing of them. Make sure he starts at the circle and follows the direction of the arrows. Concentrate on the small (not capital) letters.

Reading and writing for pleasure.

Reading and writing for pleasure.

Reading and writing for pleasure.

Reading and writing for pleasure.

These four styles show some of the most common variations used in schools. The main variations are in 'lead-in' and 'off' strokes. Odd letters, such as 'k', show different styles, but the start position and movement remain the same.

- clear printed letters, but with a 'flick' at the end to help with joining later;
- letters which have a 'lead in' and a 'lead off' stroke;
- a comprehensive lettering system, perhaps having lower case letters which all start from the base line;
- joined-up style handwriting introduced from the start.

Find out what type of paper the school uses. Children are often given unlined paper so as not to confuse or restrict their flow while the letter sizes are still large and random. However, some schools will supplement this with lined paper of varying widths, because the line can then become an aid to where your child starts a letter and to the size of each letter in relation to the lines.

Recent research suggests that there are important links between handwriting and spelling. A confident flowing style may help your child remember the look of words and the feel of writing a particular sequence of letters. Using joined writing also reduces the risks of children reversing letters and getting confused about letter order within words. Speedy, joined-up writing quite literally can help your child's flow of words and thought. It helps her concentrate and control the many different demands she faces every time she writes.

Letters can be taught in families, grouped according to their shapes. This is perhaps the most common approach. One possible pattern for this is:

- 'l', 'j', and 'i' are based on simple downward strokes, possibly with a lead-off flick;
- 'a', 'c', 'd', 'q', 'g', 'o', and 'e' follow an anti-clockwise, circular action;
- 'u' and 'y' follow a downward and curved flow;
- 'r', 'n', 'm', 'h', 'b', and 'p' start with a downward stroke being re-traced upwards;
- 'k' requires you to lift your pencil off the page to make a second 'in and out' stroke;
- 't' and 'f' require crossing, so need a second stroke too;
- 'v' and 'w' have a tricky angled start;
- 'z' and 'x' complete the angular complications!
- 's' is another loner.

These divisions, although quite logical, will not fit in with the letters your child wants to use. Her personal skills will probably blossom out of an interest in writing her own name or a desire to label things in her bedroom. She may also be encouraged to play word games and enjoy jingles which follow basic phonic links. Whatever interest your child shows, use the letters she wants and needs to write, including relevant capitals.

You want to offer your child freedom of expression. Early enthusiasm for writing is a precious gift which mustn't be trampled on. At the same time, you need to be with her often enough to notice how she is forming her letters and where she has problems which need correction. Balance your objectives so that your child is confident with her free writing yet you are not letting incorrect lettering go totally unchecked.

Helping left-handers

By the time your child starts school, you will probably have a clear idea about her hand preference. However, there are many children who seem to swap hands for different activities and are virtually ambidextrous. You may have to help determine which hand she should use, to prevent confusion once she starts school. Clarify the situation with playgroup leaders and then teaching staff as you don't want any confusion to further increase your child's difficulties. Once your child seems to have made her decision, give her your full support so that she develops a natural and comfortable writing position.

Cross-lateral children use, say, their left hand, but their right foot and eye to lead for most activities. This gives confusing signals and makes activities like copying particularly demanding. Rather like crossed telephone wires, your child must redirect the information to the appropriate side.

As a general rule, left-handers make a slower and more clumsy start to writing. The reasons for this are complicated, but they are compounded by the fact that most people teaching your child will be right-handed. There are about nine right-handers for every left-hander. As one of the privileged few myself, I sympathise with the problems faced.

PART 2: FOUNDATIONS IN SPELLING AND HANDWRITING

Hints for helping left-handers

- Offer your child equipment which is suitable for left-handers and ensure that posture and page position help establish a good style. Start by checking that the chair is high enough so she can see her work clearly.

- Some left-handers are better using a downward-sloping board for writing, although this may not be available at school.

- Do allow more space to her left so that her arm movement is unrestricted, and see that she has a comfortable, well-lit position for working.

- Next, experiment with the angle of the paper, tilting it about 30 degrees in a clockwise direction. This opens up the page for her and makes the hooked pencil hold less likely (see page 35).

- Your child will eventually find her own solutions, but observe her carefully to avoid her developing bad habits which can hinder fast flowing writing later.

  - Does the top of her pencil seem in line with her left shoulder?
  - Is her forearm parallel with top of the paper?
  - Does she hold the pencil comfortably and correctly about 2 cm from the point?

  If the answer to all these questions is 'yes', you are off to a flying start! Use a triangular pencil grip to help get correct finger positions and to avoid the vice-like hold many lefties exert! Certainly in the early stages of writing, a soft B pencil is useful as left-handers tend to push through the page. You could also encourage her to hold the paper steady with her right hand.

- Remember, your child's problems are not just with dexterity and control. She can't see what she is writing as easily as right-handers, and she will tend to smudge lettering as her hand moves across the page. Be patient with her messiness and letter reversals as these problems are far more likely to occur. However, regular praise and practice will offset natural drawbacks.

Each new stage in handwriting is likely to be more difficult for a left-hander. So when she starts to learn a new style, to join-up or to use a pen rather than a pencil, the quality of her work may suffer for a while. With time and encouragement there is no reason why she shouldn't make these transitions smoothly. (See the Appendix on page 212 for further resources and advice.) Children with particular problems with 'fine motor skills', can be helped by occupational therapy. Special programmes for your child are more likely to be successful when started early, so do speak to the school if you are worried.

Punctuation makes perfect

It takes several years for young writers to come to terms with the basic rules governing punctuation. There are so many other new skills to grapple with, quite apart from the urgency of recording ideas or developing a storyline. As with other language learning, some children tune in to punctuation relatively easily, others need patient pointing out and practice before the rudiments are there. Your child may show lovely creative ideas, and a good range of descriptive, mature language long before he perfects his punctuation.

How can I help?

Many toddlers naturally ask about strange symbols as you share books. If your child doesn't, wait until she's on the way to reading before drawing her attention to how we mark sentences with a capital letter and full stop. Reading aloud shows the logic of punctuation rules. These help you breathe, understand and add emphasis to enrich your reading.

Your child's first simple sentences in writing show her how we use punctuation. Copying your writing gives her a model and she can experiment with a word bank or sentence builder. Build up your own box of words that she often asks for and help her put

PART 2: FOUNDATIONS IN SPELLING AND HANDWRITING

st and a half

Jenny's wobbly tooth

one day Jenny awoke from her sleep. her sister
Sally was down steers eating her brekfast
her mum was dawn as well washing up
Jenny was murshling on a piece of toast
OOHH she swelled what's the matter dear
My tooth has Fallen out

Six-year-old Sophie's work is bursting with energy. The punctuation will
be worked on later.

them in the right order. This is good for learning about sentences
too as she sees how a sentence contains an idea.

Her spontaneous writing will probably be sprinkled with the
capitals she knows and attempts at using full stops. Don't worry if
this seems completely random at first. At least she knows what
markers she must include: where to put them takes much longer.

By seven your child is expected to write simple sentences correctly most of the time, using full stops, capitals and question marks
appropriately. You can help draw out this awareness during reading
sessions, where the text is more complex and reflects a wider range
of punctuation. Her spontaneous writing will include dialogue and
questions, so introduce symbols as the need arises. This can be
backed up with 'punctuation spotting' as you read. Make deliberate
mistakes and get her to explain what punctuation is needed.

Get into the habit of proof-reading and editing aloud, so she can hear her own mistakes. Punctuation mistakes are easily overlooked because your child knows what she wants to say. Getting someone else to read her work 'cold' highlights any problems. Don't do this too often, and only with older, experienced writers who have the confidence and experience to understand what corrections they need to make. Share editing with younger ones, gently pointing out incorrect or missed punctuation, and noting problem areas to tackle later.

The wonders of workbooks to practise English skills?

Most parents find concise, checklist-style workbooks, covering basic grammar and spelling rules, very attractive. Children may have different ideas! I have suggested a few series worth investigating in the Appendix on page 220, but here are some of the points to consider:

- Will he work regularly from it? Is there enough motivation? Everyone varies: some children enjoy straightforward exercises where they can easily check their own progress, others find these sterile and switch off. They need a lively format, colour pages and questions, quizzes or puzzles to hold their interest.
- Checklists give you a result by which to measure your child's progress. But there are problems. The exercises may not actually reach the skills you intend to test. It may be possible for your child to copy the formula of the exercise, rather than to have to apply her knowledge. Such tests are by nature different to real writing although they can help her confidence, concentration and study skills.
- Other series use an open-ended approach, requiring your child to create answers and propose solutions. These are sharing, thinking and 'talking about' books, rather than quick individual exercises to check skills. Many have an attractive colour layout but are more costly than plain test books. How-

PART 2: FOUNDATIONS IN SPELLING AND HANDWRITING

ever, they often give excellent advice and ideas for further activities. They may be able to turn dry information into something to which your child can relate.

CHAPTER SEVEN

Starting to read alone

Signs of progress

It's a tremendous relief when you realise your child is really on the road to becoming a reader. Rather like those first real words that she spoke as a toddler, it may not be easy always to define exactly when your child becomes a reader. This depends partly on what you mean by reading. Do you count using the pictures, reading very familiar books and guessing? I have tried to show that all these skills are valuable and important to a young reader.

You'll want the reassurance that your child can start to enjoy new books confidently on her own. Despite this target, we have to train ourselves to be patient. The early stages of reading need sensitive handling, so your child must not feel rushed or pressured. Apart from the fact that she needs to practise her skills at one level before rising to the challenges of the next, she should have time to enjoy her own success. Think about what you read for pleasure, and the message is the same: you don't always reach for something demanding and complex. In fact you may deliberately avoid a challenging novel in favour of a quick browse through a magazine or the indulgence of re-reading your favourite author. Your child needs time to relax with familiar, 'easy' books as these old favourites will have a special quality for her which we must respect.

Sticking to a scheme?

School reading schemes offer the comfort of a clear structure by which you can measure your child's progress. This yardstick is dangerous and misleading if you come to regard it as the main evidence that your child is a reader. Real readers aren't confined to a set diet and format. While these schemes give your child chances for success and security, he needs your help to gain the confidence to apply his new skills to a wide range of reading material. Some children find this very difficult as they don't like the uncertainty. If you have always shared books together, and encouraged your child to guess confidently when tackling new words, he will more readily adapt to new formats. Of course, many schools recognise this and use a variety of schemes from the start. Flexibility and sensitivity are the key words at this stage. Fledgling readers deserve our time and support.

Keeping involved with school reading

Most schools continue to send home reading books regularly, although the pace may slacken once your child is off the early-reading stage. The books she's reading will become longer and she may not need as much support. Don't reduce your involvement unless you feel shut out by your little silent reader. Respect her desire for privacy as she enjoys her new skills, but invite her to share sessions too. Ask her to explain about books she brings back from school and to read favourite passages to you.

Use any diary system which accompanies school reading books; record your child's reactions, note any difficulties and raise issues. Often you will just want to write 'enjoyed' or give the page numbers you read, but do let the teacher know your child's attitude to these sessions, particularly if you are concerned. She may, for example, always want you to read the book through first. This is fine as long as she seems happy to take some part in a second or third reading. If she seems bored or reluctant, again it is better to discuss this with the teacher than to jeopardise your relaxed reading enjoyment at home.

All children go through phases, and it's easy to get anxious before allowing sufficient time for the problem to resolve itself naturally. You are not being pushy or fussy by voicing concerns with your child's teacher sooner rather than later. Brooding worries can harm the delicate balance you have built with your child. The knowledge that both you and the school are working together lends support and confidence.

Too easy or too hard

You may not always agree with the level of the reading books sent home, and will get itchy if the same book comes home day after day. Find out who is choosing the books. If your child wants to read something repeatedly, she may need to for a while. If the teachers wants a book re-read because your child is struggling, then this should be made clear to you. Enjoying familiar books is a positive part of being a reader, but struggling repeatedly over a book which holds little interest is a different matter. On the other hand, your child may need frequent chances to re-read to boost his confidence.

> ❝ He reads quite well but lacks confidence and is frightened of making mistakes. ❞

However, teachers are only human! They do make mistakes, and they do have to deal with about 30 little readers, not just one. They can't always be aware of your child's reactions to a book, nor notice what she may be sneaking home in her folder. Help communication by pointing concerns out without getting rattled or showing your frustration. By keeping the focus on your child's reactions rather than your own judgement about reading material or your child's rate of progress, you will invite calm conversation rather than defensive remarks.

If worries persist, arrange a meeting with the teacher, instead of vying for her attention during the hubbub at the end of the school day. If possible, arrange for your children to be elsewhere, so you can talk freely. Make a list of the key issues you want covered, and the reasons for your concern. Try to get concrete examples of what the teacher wants you to be doing at home and work out a clear programme for dealing with any problems.

Working parents

The days of lingering over the cloakroom pegs are well and truly over. Your child skips off happily through the school gates, and emerges from the same spot about six hours later. Perhaps you drop her off on the way to work and arrange for a friend or relative to pick her up in the afternoon. Whatever arrangement you make, it's a juggling act and there is little scope for relaxed chats with the class teacher.

Your contact may be less direct and confined to evenings or days off, but teachers are sensitive to your desire to be involved. Do go along to special meetings and take up initiatives made by the school to keep you informed. Aim for regular, if brief, contact with the teacher through notes and arranged meetings after school. Ask for examples of your child's work, reading activities and class games to be shown, or perhaps borrowed over a weekend. Talk to other parents and keep a very clear vision of the wide range of reading experiences you want to offer your child at home. It is even more important when there is a physical distance that you exploit the channels of communication with the school to their full effect. If in doubt about something, seek assurance through a brief meeting, or try to get something in writing.

Six-year-old Letitia has a good understanding of *Not Now Bernard* by David McKee. Her script reads: Not Now Bernard. Bernard went down stairs into the lounge. He went outside he saw a monster in the garden (in the garden). Bernard went to the monster the monster looked at Bernard. The End.

Perfect timing

As you get more involved in after-school activities, juggling swimming, Beavers and karate with the weekly shopping, reading time gets squeezed. Guard against this retreat if you can, by creating a regular space for reading together. In an ideal world, there would always be those relaxed ten minutes without background noise, cats to feed and babies to settle. But a workable solution, which you can all enjoy, needs its feet firmly planted in the real world. It is the atmosphere you create when reading which is more important than how many words you actually cover.

How do I help my child cope with unfamiliar words?

The pattern for sharing reading outlined on page 44 is useful once your child is starting to read independently. She will benefit from the chance to flip through the book first, or even to listen to you as you read it. It is tempting to sit back and wait to be read to once you know she can do it, but this could undermine the trust and relaxed enjoyment you have worked so hard to establish.

Take the hints your child offers as she will soon fend you off when she wants to read alone straight away. She needs to feel your involvement is still supportive and focused on enjoying books rather than on testing her skills.

When your child gets stuck on a word, give her time to use the information available to her. As before, if she's getting distressed, it's better to give her the word and perhaps explain how the sentence, word order or letter sound helped you. As her confidence grows, so should her willingness to guess, even if the word she offers isn't correct. How you deal with this will influence her readiness to try alone later.

- Focus her attention on the clues (or cues) offered. This could be as simple as pointing to the picture.

Alternatively say:

- 'That's a tricky word. Let's see if we can guess it by reading that sentence again.'
- 'What word makes sense there? Let's read to the end and see if we can fit one in.'
- 'What sound is at the beginning of the word?'
- 'What word looks right there?'

All these questions invite your child to use different strategies to make an informed guess. You would not need to draw the alternatives out every time, but could guide her to trying different approaches until she offers words and ideas of her own.

If she substitutes a word which makes sense, accept it. When you reach the end of the page you could praise her word whilst pointing out that the author chose something different. Look more closely at the shape and initial sounds of the word to help her accuracy.

What about sounding out the word?

Using our knowledge of letter sounds and patterns is just one important aid to reading new words. You could read my nonsense word 'splation' because you are familiar with how to pronounce such groups of letters, but that doesn't help you understand them. Keep in mind the main purpose of reading, that we should make sense of print, and you'll appreciate the need to 'apply but not rely' on grapho-phonic knowledge. Besides, English is awash with words which don't fit the rules, so your child needs other skills too.

Do encourage your child to look closely at the start of words and to use the visual pattern and sound links to good effect. You can help by making the sounds clearly, helping him become aware of blends and groups of sounds. 'Phonemic awareness' refers to the ability to hear and segment words, to build up words through their parts like a sounds jigsaw. Some children acquire this skill more readily than others, but taking time to help your child in this way when she actually needs it, is extremely useful.

Making meaning

Help your child open up her approach to reading by using what she knows already to tackle the unfamiliar. This involves re-reading, leaving a gap and reading on, so that she sees what type of word would make sense. It also requires thinking about the flow of the story, the message offered by pictures, and the knowledge she already has. This last point is important. All those years of answering the tormenting questions 'why', and the hours that you have spent talking about and sharing books, give your child a database to work from. This allows her to use semantic information to make sense of what she is reading through focusing on the meaning and what she expects the words to say.

What about flashcards?

Fluent readers need to recognise words automatically, to have a good sight vocabulary. This can't be easily achieved through looking at words in isolation, but through reading itself. You can, of course, back up her reading through playing games with words that she will find useful. There are also those dull but essential 'joining' words which need to be remembered. This should happen naturally if your child meets such words regularly in her reading. You can help by pointing out words, matching and writing out as you read together. If you want to use flashcards, use them in games and as aids to shared writing sessions. Some children enjoy the challenge of remembering words, or the satisfaction of showing off their skills, but be sensitive to your child's attitude. Look back at earlier suggestions such as word bingo, lotto and dominoes, and adapt these to match your child's ability.

Lastly, think about the order of words in sentences. Encourage your child to use her knowledge of spoken English to fit in words which sound right. You will know from learning a second language, or from grappling with a European language on your holidays, that word order isn't standard!

Don't lose your temper!

It is frustrating when your child reads a word effortlessly on one page and then stumbles over it the next. It's doubly trying if you've just spent five minutes working through ways to guess that word! The connection seems logical to us, but your child has lots of fresh and tentative information to juggle in her head. It's inevitable that slips will sometimes occur.

Perhaps you feel she's not concentrating or trying. At this stage it would be better to call a halt until you both feel fresh and positive again. You are unlikely to achieve lasting results by sticking it out, and you risk blowing a fuse yourself! Beat a fairly subtle retreat before steam fumes from your ears. Simply offer the correct words, explain the connection and confess your own tiredness. Then back off, and relax doing something completely different.

How do I know which books to choose

Which books will match my child's ability?

You want to offer your child a wide and stimulating range of books, stories, poetry and information books, but where do you start? Any visit to a book shop or library offers a confusing array of early readers. The Appendix on page 220 offers lists of popular books, together with sources of information to keep you up to date.

You still need a good selection of picture books with words as well as books without words. Starting to read doesn't mean neglecting the beauty and value of these books. Choose books with your child, letting her tastes and interests steer you. Balance this by looking for books by authors you know are successful, responding to advice from teachers, librarians and book clubs. The acid test is that your child will want to read it!

This is a difficult stage because you don't want to damage early confidence by offering her books which are too difficult, but you do want to provide challenging and rewarding material.

When you are reading together, take a mental note of how frequently your child makes mistakes or is unable to read a word. If one word in ten trips her up, this is definitely a book you should be reading mainly to her. She may want to share in the reading, from echoing your words to filling in during a second or third reading, but leaving her to struggle alone would cause frustration.

If she only makes mistakes every one in 15 words, then you could offer to support her reading. Only if the mistakes occur at ratio of about one in 25 should you feel happy to let her read alone. Even then, it is always best to preview the story together, and perhaps read a few key words before she goes solo.

Qualities to look for in first reading books

These figures provide some guidance, but are hard to relate to everyday choosing and reading. Besides, you'll want to respect her growing desire for independence when browsing through books. If she really wants to borrow a book which you know is far too difficult, let her take it. Explain you would love to share it with her, and then offer as much support as she needs and you are allowed to give!

The challenge for authors is to provide sharp, stimulating stories which have pace and which reflect young readers' interests without being patronising. The books need to have solid, strong characters who move through a fast-moving plot, yet are not glib and shallow. The content makes demands upon the reader, even if the vocabulary and number of words are limited. Not surprisingly, this balance is far from easy to achieve.

Several read-alone series are worth investigating. The better ones use quality authors who provide different styles of writing in attractive and manageable formats. Such titles offer a bridge between picture books and longer novels, being broken down into pages containing only a few sentences and good illustrations.

The attraction for both you and your child is that a series allows you to choose from a range which matches his ability level. Having had success with one title, your child may look for the same design because he feels confident of coping. A young reader tends to be very loyal. If he gets a taste for an author, he will go on to try more demanding books by the same person. A word of warning though: judge each title on its own merits and look for subject matter that will tempt your child. Like earlier school readers, these books should complement picture books and any longer stories your child is drawn to, not take their place. (See the Appendix on page 220.)

Initially look for the same features talked about when choosing picture books:

- a strong, interesting storyline with a clear sequence;
- rhythm, rhyme and repetition to help predict the text;
- pictures on every page, and clear print, larger than in a full-sized novel;
- the text and the pictures work together;
- familiar authors and subjects.

Then look more closely at the text:

- There should be only a few sentences on each page, so that they aren't daunting.
- The language should be familiar and lively.
- Look for subjects which interest your child, which have humour, silly jokes, a twist in the tail or a serious message which is relevant to your child.
- The book must look good, with zany or detailed illustrations designed to hook little readers. Explore different styles together, including comic strip and puzzle-solving types. Text which uses dialogue and a variety of typefaces is more likely to appeal than unbroken text.

Keep reading!

As long as you have a willing audience, keep reading! What comes naturally at the toddler stage is worth preserving for as long as possible. By reading aloud, you help her dip into more demanding texts, to meet new language structures and to get ideas to help her

PART 3: STARTING TO READ ALONE

I like Snowy because
I like the colours.
of Snowey I like
the feather's on
Him I like the job
He has to do

Nicola's response to *Snowy*, reminds us of the lasting beauty of picture books.

own powers of expression. Don't expect your child to read to you with much expression yet: these separate skills can be encouraged later. For now most of her energies will be required just to make sense of the text. Talking about the books you encounter helps your child become an active reader who evaluates and questions as she reads. These skills may take years to establish, but talking shows that reading is an active process, that we explore new ideas yet can also question and criticise how something has been written. Prompt conversation by saying things like 'I wonder why the girl decided to do that?', 'I'd be terrified if that happened', 'I thought that was a really funny ending' . . .

Ask your child which characters she liked, what she found amusing or sad and what she thought of the outcome. Look at the pictures and presentation critically too, encouraging more than a one-word response.

In what other ways can I help with reading?

Reading will of course feature in your day-to-day activities. As her competence grows, so your child can participate more fully. This will include reading the television schedule to book her favourites, noting reminders about things to take to school, and requests for new clothes. She will also enjoy sorting the post and reading her own mail, so encourage friends and relations to keep up a regular correspondence.

Use reading to direct creative tasks, from cooking to modelling and building. Although she may need support, there is a great sense of achievement in following instructions correctly to make something which actually works.

Follow TV trends and peer pressure if they involve your child in enjoying reading. There is nothing dangerous about comics (in fact there are a few of very high quality) or books which emerge from programmes and films. Some are, admittedly, far better written than others, but it's natural for your child to relish the popular appeal of these titles. Strike a balance early, accepting her choice yet guiding her to a range of other reading material as well. She will probably develop creative play ideas from these film and TV characters, so they will help her language grow in other ways.

Story tapes are another valuable resource. Again, some are vastly superior to others in how they are produced. Offer a range, from those which are tightly tied to a text and which have blips to tell your child when to move on to the next page, to those which are a listening theatre, complete with different voices and entertaining sound effects. Tapes help concentration, introduce challenging stories and invite fresh interpretations of old favourites. They emphasise the relaxing luxury of books and the escapism they offer. Conversely, book and tape sets concentrate on following the words, perhaps reading along or introducing a story before your child tries to read the book alone. They don't compete with shared reading time, but offer an alternative independent approach for story-lovers. They serve as a reminder of the power of storytelling to entertain and educate.

Word games and activity books

Both of these have a value for fledgling readers, particularly when matched to your child's interests and viewed as a shared activity rather than something to keep her quiet.

I Spy Anywhere, Anytime, Anyhow . . .

It's as old as the hills but children love it, and you can create infinite varieties to suit your circumstances. So while at home, try giving initial sound clues for your child to guess what's hidden in a box or under a tea towel. Use the same technique to give clues about the position of some buried treasure (smarties are usually popular). Give instructions for an action game by asking her to perform something beginning with 'I'. Similarly, get her chasing around the house fetching objects beginning with a certain sound. If the mood takes you, you can then create a nonsense tongue-twister based on the objects in front of you. Writing down offers a further link to jolt her memory.

Word power

Word attack skills are important for independent readers and have obvious links with spelling and writing. Much can be achieved through shared writing activities, but continue with word memory and matching games to help her confidence and quick recall.

Alphabet matching game

Explain the value of distinguishing letter sounds, and make your own alphabet matching game. Write out the lower case letters on cards and use pictures or drawings of familiar objects to make the clue cards. Catalogues showing alphabet puzzles, and picture dictionaries, offer sources of inspiration.

Making a game like this with your child offers learning opportunities with a real sense of purpose. If you look critically at some puzzles, you'll notice how misleading they can be: many include clues like 'frog' and 'tree' which start with a blend of sounds rather than 'telephone' and 'fire' which give clear initial sounds. If you talk about this as you make the game, your child's understanding will increase.

Once you have made the game, try matching the pairs against the clock, or playing it as a memory game. Make sure your child concentrates on the initial sounds, then write out the names of the objects she has correctly identified and place them in alphabetical order.

When your child is familiar with this game, use the same cards as a basis for bingo, lotto and sound snap using a tape recording of letter sounds.

Magnetic letters

Magnetic letters are a good source for letter and word games without the additional strain of writing. Make word snakes where the last letter of one word is used as the first letter of the next. Start at the top of the fridge door, and see if you can create words in a step formation all the way to the floor.

A rainbow arch of letters in alphabetical order is a good sequence tester. Let your child hide your eyes as you remove one, then see how quickly she can spot what's gone. As she gets quicker, remove two at a time, and increase the number of letters used. When you play this game, make the letter sounds first and then refer back to the letter names (see page 23).

Magnetic letters making up 3 words: 'cat', 'tap' and 'peg'.

If your child enjoyed labelling games when she was younger, adopt the approach using whole phrases. Positional phrases such as 'on top', 'under' and 'behind' give clues for finding hidden objects, or instructions for where your child should go to find the next clue. Rewards, whether verbal, confectionery or concrete, add a real sense of purpose. After all, reading has functional value as well as leisure pleasure.

CHAPTER EIGHT

On the write tracks

There are so many different skills to master in the early phases of reading and writing that it's hard to know where to focus your attention. With so much else to squeeze into a busy day, how can you create room for writing?

Room for writing

Spellings and handwriting support can be very useful. But the best basis for your home help lies through creative play and writing messages for real people. A real purpose for writing provides a reason for sorting through spelling and presentation problems together.

Teachers show great initiative in creating situations at school which offer their pupils a reason for their writing, and which give each child some sense of personal control over their work. However, this has to be balanced with writing book exercises, story sessions, simple comprehension and project work. To a considerable extent the teacher's hands are tied; she may have a class of over 30 and a tight curriculum schedule to meet. So she can't allow your child the time and attention to follow his own interests. Your home, despite the other activities you cram into each day, does offer personal freedom of time and expression, with the potential to develop your child's interests more fully. Having said that, many other activities compete for his time and writing can be a laborious, slow process.

So how do I help?

Be a writer yourself. As with reading, your child will value a skill more readily if he sees you at it. Don't save letter writing, lists and note-taking until the evening.

In the same way as the jacket to a book makes you want to read it, writing is easier if it looks attractive. Gradually build up an assortment of material to interest your child. Greater choice and variety will give your child more power over his productions. It's amazing how a dinosaur-shaped notelet or a magic writing pen can tempt reluctant writers.

A desk, table or comfortable place for writing is also important. It may be that your child loves scrawling over the chaos on the kitchen table, where he feels warm and in the thick of things. Alternatively, he might want to cocoon himself away, or use his toys as part of his writing. His reason for his writing will probably dictate where he works and what he needs, but having things to hand makes it easier to respond to a sudden whim.

Your attention and support are the greatest assets. Make the most of them now, before he slinks off, rehearsing his teenage 'I want to do my own thing' role at ten! It isn't always easy to get the balance between inviting and persuading, but a reluctant child is unlikely to make lasting progress. How you respond to her writing will play a key role in your child's attitude and self-confidence.

An attitude problem?

This is always a difficult area to deal with, but start by re-assessing your own. If you remember writing activities as being stressful, time-consuming and divorced from your real interests, it will be hard to enthuse your child. By encouraging her to write indepen-

HELP YOUR CHILD WITH READING AND WRITING

Thursday 6th Jan

myroom. my room is nise. my room has ~~blue~~ blue curtains and I have got a doll that is Sally secrets. my bed has got a patchwork quilt and Toms has got a patch work quilt as well at night I have a glass of milk and mum ses good night and I

go to sleep the end *
6 lpm.

one day when me and Tom where in the play room playing with Tracey Bland mummy siad les go to The prk. So me and Tom whent to the park. mummy siad Shall we let Lauren Come as well He and Tom siad ok. it will OK ~~wo~~ wontit.

Thursday 6th January

my bed roam

In my bed roam I have a pretty quilt on my bed. I liked my quilt. My quilt was from my Nana. My curtains are green. and My wall paper is white. my Carpet is pink ✓ b lon. good *

Monday 10th January Lauro

on Sunday I went to mathews house for tea I had chip's for tea. I liked my tea and I Watched TV and Oliver was there. Oliver went to bed. Oliver is my brother ✓
10 lor

Playtimes, bedrooms and chips for tea are all reasons for writing!

dently and to concentrate on real issues or real people, you offer a purpose and freedom.

Manageable proportions

Give your child simple, practical reasons for writing, like adding to the family shopping list, ordering juice from the milkman or choosing her favourite video for the weekend. A white-board or space for notices in the kitchen, which everyone uses, could help get her started.

When she shows *any* interest offer as much help, spellings and support as she needs. Some children aren't happy to write alone when they know 'it isn't right', and it's very hard to shift this attitude. If your child wants to copy out your writing at least this is a start and she will learn from watching you. As soon as you can, ease her on to creating writing for herself.

> ❝ *That's not right!*
> ❝ *Lovely, but how about if you . . .*

A reluctant writer demands a particularly sympathetic audience, yet one whose message and praise is sincere. If your first objective is to get her enjoying writing, concentrate on motivation rather than correction.

> ❝ *If she needs spellings I give them without too much fuss. Now that she's enjoying it, she's gone from strength to strength.*
>
> (Parent with nine-year-old daughter)

The more she does, the more chances you have to encourage and help her.

What is emergent writing and how can it help my child

Emergent or free writing refers to writing done completely unaided. It offers control to young writers from the start, and freedom from the reliance on adult support. All children need the experience of free writing and it gives unique insights into what they actually know about writing through seeing what they can apply for themselves. For most children this is a liberating experience, but for a

HELP YOUR CHILD WITH READING AND WRITING

Goldilosks and the three Bears
One day a girl was walking in the forest.
When Goldilocks came To a cottage in the woods
the cottage was foll of colours there were
red orange yellow green and Blue The Bears
Came Back from there walk They saw
Goldilocks in there cottage up stairs
In there bad room Goldilocks tymped out of
the Window. and the Bears hever saw Goldilocks
again

7.9.93.

This talented six-year-old's retelling of Goldilocks shows the accuracy of her own spelling, her lively language and sense of story structure. We should note, but not criticise, her lettering and punctuation.

few it is fraught with anxieties. The earlier your child is offered such opportunities, the more likely she will be to respond.

❝ *But I can't read a word of it!* ❞

Studies of free writing have unearthed a clear pattern in how most children learn to write. Once the logic of each phase is clear, it's possible to crack the code. Very young children scribble in a way which reflects their knowledge of print. So at first there may be odd symbols used, perhaps a row of squiggles which repeat a pattern. Later there could be gaps between the patterns. Although they aren't conventional letters, these shapes act like words in the way that they flow across the page and your toddler would be able to tell

PART 3: ON THE WRITE TRACKS

you what her writing says. She may experiment with different 'lettering', just like the variety of print she sees all around her. She will
also refine her writing to show that the words come in different
shapes and sizes. Eventually actual letters will creep in, often those
of her name making a star appearance.

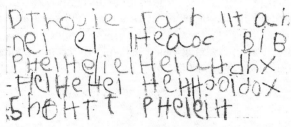

This five-year-old has started school already showing what she knows about
writing.

   The more examples of writing she sees around her and the more
openings her play offers for writing, the more quickly she is likely
to refine her skills.

This shows a clear marking of words through using initial sounds. It says
'I went to Poole Mummy bought me a mask.'

HELP YOUR CHILD WITH READING AND WRITING

Invented spelling in school-age children still follows a clear logic. Her increasing knowledge of writing is reflected. To begin with, letters 'mark' the words they represent as she focuses on the start and ending sounds using her growing sound/symbol knowledge. The teacher will be enriching your child's understanding through a diet of applied phonics, reading and handwriting. As new awareness filters through to her writing, you will see more sounds and parts of words being represented. She will attempt vowels and more tricky letter combinations but will, of course, sometimes muddle and confuse the rules.

Now the endings of words are represented and familiar words like 'the' are written correctly. This says: 'Sonic the hedgehog is speeding everywhere.'

A closer look at her work shows how rapidly she progresses through these stages. However, she is dealing with a complex language system that is full of quirks and pitfalls. For instance, she will probably use letter names rather than letter sounds to help her spell. The letter 'y' is therefore used to represent the sound 'why', giving spelling like 'yet' (went) and 'yuts' (once). She tries to mark every sound with a letter, but has yet to appreciate silent letters, letters which combine to make one new sound (such as 'ph') and the complexity of vowel sounds.

Perhaps your child is a phonemic speller. She will be able to say

Hurry The

exscvators

r cumming

Notice 'r' for 'are' and the spelling of 'excavators'.

the word to herself, and break it down into manageable blocks of sound. To produce just one word she must repeat the mental process again and again, concentrating on each sound in turn. Like 'sounding out' in reading, the logic of this often fails to produce the correct word. As your reader matures, so her writing will show an appreciation of some of the rules and conventions which govern spelling and writing. Unfortunately, a prolific reader isn't necessarily a good speller.

How long will it take for her to write properly?

This is very individual and depends to a large extent on what she could do when she started school, but your child will be taught ways to help her spell, and should also have a growing stock of common words she has memorised by age six. Her free writing should show what rules she can't use correctly, indicating where attention is needed. Help her value her writing, and support her developing skills through playing word games together.

HELP YOUR CHILD WITH READING AND WRITING

odAm was escbat id it was christmas eve he had
put his sdoking at the botsme ove his bed, he had
a christmas tree too. In the moning he looks in his
sdoking he sore a Dunsor and adragne angaban ove
choklite. his brover got a rabbit. and his sister got
a orange.

Lauren pulfer 6½

Six-year-old Lauren shows both confidence and sophistication. You can see how rules, remembered spellings and phonemic awareness are working towards a readable message. (Clues to help with translation: excited, stocking, of, dinosaur and brother!)

> But my child would be given the impression that he can write when he can't.

It depends how you define writing. Writing isn't much use if it can't be read by others (although even young scribblers can share their ideas). If your child accepts this and has real people who want to

PART 3: ON THE WRITE TRACKS

read his writing, he will more readily re-draft and correct his own work. Drafting is the logical bridge between free and conventional writing.

Emergent writing works from the opposite end of the scale to more conventional methods of early writing, because it concentrates first on the whole process of writing and on the free flow of ideas. Writing is about having something worthwhile to say and, if you don't get stuck on each word, the satisfaction of creating can be very strong.

Once upon a time there was a lady a very poor lady. She had no money She only a Garden that day It was Snowing and she belt a Snowman. She did not have a man in the house. Becaucase he went to live Somewhere else to live. So the lady lived. on her own.

Jade's story is both readable and touching.

Conversely, copy writing, dictionaries, word-books and lists focus on the parts, on producing the words accurately, and on building up the whole. As with reading methods, both approaches can be harmonised to some extent, allowing your child to play to his own strengths. Children are acutely aware of their own shortfalls regarding spelling and presentation, so will often respond to offers of help. If they value what they are working for they are usually eager to correct and re-write their work.

HELP YOUR CHILD WITH READING AND WRITING

one nit a lilk mouse wos wokn Hy a sran nos
hiy got up and la a rad the hasy
the nos got lad and lad and lad
the mouse wos geti a hedak
hiy pot his pillow ov his hed
tent the nos got cwit and cwit and cwit
tent the mouse wet to slip

Six-year-old Emma's story shows humour and a writer's talent for pacing.
(One night a little mouse was woken by a strange noise. He got up and
looked around the house. The noise got louder and louder and louder.
The mouse was getting a headache. He put his pillow over his head then
the noise got quieter and quieter and quieter then the mouse went to sleep.)

Making methods work

Most schools use a combination of approaches and it should be
fairly easy to blend the methods to suit your child. Talk to his
teacher, and get clear guidelines as to what your school does, then
take the lead from your child. Make the technique you use work
for your child: that's what counts. The approach used should also
be appropriate to the purpose for writing: a fan's letter to his football
club should be posted with pride, a personal reminder to watch
'Grange Hill' is thrown in the bin once you've switched on.

Other ways you can help

Most early writing deals with your child's immediate, egocentric
ideas. As she matures, she will need to tackle different types of
writing assignment. Here are some practical ways to help:

- Encourage her observation skills, talking, describing and
  comparing things that capture her interest when you are out
  walking. Playing 'feely' games requires her to put sensations
  into words, and by recording this you can test out her accu-

racy, seeing if she can match back the object of her own description.

- Help her to report a sequence of events accurately, putting things in order. Again, this can be done orally, through pictures or by you jotting down her words. Try these activities to help her:
  - Ask her to give you clear instructions how to make or build something. The end result will speak for itself and highlight the importance and difficulty of recording clearly and accurately.
  - A sense of order is important for story writing too. When you read together, discuss the start, build-up and conclusion. Talking about characters focuses on the detail which brings them to life.

How much can she write?

❝ I've written three pages! ❞

Bear in mind that your child is only just coming to terms with writing in whole sentences. She may sometimes get carried away with her thoughts, but the end result seems full of repetition, a string of ideas linked by 'and then . . . and then'. At this stage many children get a great sense of achievement from covering pages, or from going onto a new page for the first time. Even when your child's writing is enlarged, or her sentences are remarkably similar, we should share her sense of success for a while. Remembering the complexity of writing, this is still an achievement. Quality as well as volume plays its part in her progress, but every writer counts her words!

For those who haven't caught the page-count bug, offer a support or framework to get them started. Lists, messages and letters set their own limits, but you can do this with more creative writing too. Rather like poetry, nursery rhymes and early picture books, repeating a series of words or offering the start of a sentence gives your child a foothold. For example, build up sentences around a colour theme:

> 'Blue is the shining sea, blue is the summer sky, blue is a forget-me-not and blue is Dad's tie.'

Alternatively, give a starting point:

> 'Crash! my bike hit the rock and . . .'

The words you use will reflect those which come naturally in everyday conversation.

Talking and sharing opinions is a crucial part of writing. Once hooked on an idea, your child will show you how much support she needs. She may want to dash off her own thoughts and then discuss things with you later, or she might prefer to talk through each stage with you first. If you can spare the time, respond to these requests to boost her confidence.

As with beginner readers, your writer needs careful nurturing. A diet of praise, purpose, prompts and practice should be tailored to suit her needs.

PART 3: ON THE WRITE TRACKS

Christopher

Happiness

Happiness is bright orange.

The taste of happiness is like warm rice pudding.

Smelling of cheese and tomato pizza.

It looks like a lively street with children playing in it.

The sounds of happiness are people singing.

Happiness feels like fun.

13th Sept 93

If my thoughts took shape

If my happy thoughts came
to life,
They would be someone having
a wonderful surprise,
just like hundred balloons rising
in the sky.

If my sad thoughts took shape,
They would be like,
a baby crying and a mother
doing nothing about it.

If my suspicious thoughts
took shape,
They would be like,
lights coming on in a empty
house.

If my Mysterious thoughts
took shape,
They would be like,
Hurtly lakes of water lying
in a flower covered valley.

If my furious thoughts took
shape,
They would be like,
People fighting without reason.

If my fearless thoughts
took shape,
They would be like,
a person walking through
fire covered in petrol

Excellent. A very descriptive poem. Well done

A simple framework produced magic results with these older juniors.

CHAPTER NINE

Racing or reading?

Between the ages of seven and nine, most children are in the process of refining their reading skills and of enjoying some degree of independence. Learning to read doesn't stop once the early and most obvious hurdles have been jumped. Ideally we mature and develop as readers throughout our lives. Enjoying and valuing reading for its own sake offers your child the best chance of discovering this for herself. Although it's difficult to squeeze in, ten minutes reading every night could provide the basis for a life-long habit. This could mean a snuggle with books before bed, or a session relaxing after tea when you both still have the energy. Whatever works for you both.

Read to me!

Continue to offer regular times for enjoying books together. If this is impossible because you are not wanted, or because you don't have the time any more, think how you could reach a compromise. Try reading snippets of more demanding books, or interesting her in some of the excellent story tapes, media tie-ins and story selections available.

Powers of expression or deception?

Reading aloud is an art and not all of us enjoy this theatrical role. If you don't, perhaps your partner or another adult would be willing to share their skill with your child. Similarly, your child may not enjoy reading aloud to you. If this is the case, talk about her reading together and offer to re-read sections for her to aid your discussion. Occasionally, suggest that she rehearses and then reads a couple of favourite passages to you. Take the pressure off these sessions, but offer her constructive tips about using punctuation, pacing and varying her expression once she is reading aloud more regularly.

Some children have silver tongues and glide through readings with wonderful expression and sense of timing. If you are lucky enough to listen to such performances from your child, do tactfully check that she also understands what she's reading. It is easy to get fooled by the magic of their voice! We read because we want to make sense of something, but when you read aloud you are concentrating on different skills too. It is quite possible for readers to switch off, to forget words and ideas almost the instant they've been read. Time spent reading aloud needs to be matched by time spent discussing the content.

My child reads like a robot. It's hard to stay awake.

Perhaps the books he is choosing are too difficult for him. He's using all his energies to make sense of the words and has little space left for frills or deeper understanding. Tempt him to read an easier, amusing book with plenty of dialogue. You could try reading a play together, or a simple text with strong dramatic emphasis. If he's reading things that interest him, he's more likely to respond to their meaning.

My child only wants to read to herself. Half the time, I haven't a clue what she's reading.

As the books get longer and your child is increasingly influenced by outside forces when she chooses what to read, it is harder to gain a foothold. This should be easier to resolve if you have always had a sharing, pleasurable involvement in her reading. To get over her reluctance to read aloud, offer to read to her or try a technique like paired reading (which is described on page 131).

One trick is to get yourself informed and to use the experience of experts in helping your child choose books. Compromise becomes the keyword: you should accept her choices and hope she tackles yours with an open mind. We tend to limit the range of literature we want children to read, concentrating on what we see as proper books. Comics, media books and light relief series all have adult parallels, so why are they necessarily damaging for our children? A reading habit is more important than what's being read. It gives a platform for change, influence and the discovery of fantastic books. The best you can do is to show him the rich variety of material available. Being informed and interested in discussing his choice of reading shows your child you care and provides an opening into his reading world.

Keeping up with the kids: Sources of information about children's books

Your local library may produce pamphlets designed for different ages, interests and reading levels. If they are not visible, do ask, as such material can often be obtained for you. I collected these examples from my area:

- picture books, including a selection for older readers;
- a borrower's card for six- to eight-year-olds, with ten top authors to track down. You have your card stamped once you've read the book. A borrower's badge gives an added incentive to read all ten!
- a feedback system encouraging children to vote for their favourite book;

- leaflets responding to current trends, such as dinosaur mania;
- ten of the best, a list of classics and modern greats for the independent reader;
- 'Wicked Ace Brill' books – not to be missed for older readers of around twelve.

If your branch library is very small, contact the county children's librarian for information.

Specialist children's bookshops or a good children's department of a larger store are a wealth of knowledge to those lucky enough to have such a perk close by. Talk to other parents and teachers to find out about your local provision.

There are many other organisations with a wealth of knowledge and enthusiasm. Tap into this by referring to details listed in the Appendix on pages 212–219.

From browsing to selecting a good book

As a thoroughly informed parent, you can suggest a few choice authors when you're next browsing together. Not all children take time choosing books. Even keen readers can whirl through the shelves picking up the first attractive cover which catches their eye, refusing any invitation to open and sample before borrowing. Talking time is again the main solution. Look at the jacket and show your child where to find the blurb, then flick through the pages and try to guess something about the content. If your child finds this difficult, play it like a game together, guessing the starting point before reading the first chapter to see if you are right.

Having got an overview, test-read the first couple of pages to see whether the reading level fits. Pleasure reading shouldn't be too demanding, although it is often challenging. Your child may be desperate to read something recommended by a friend, or be drawn to a difficult book because she likes the author or subject-matter. Her gritty determination should ensure success. Do help out with some shared reading so she can complete the book in a reasonable time and gain confidence from finishing a 'thick' book. If possible, steer her to a lighter read if she frequently opts for books which seem slightly above her comfortable reading level. (See pages 90 and 96.) Find poetry selections, funny books and short stories which she might enjoy listening to as well.

Becoming a critical reader

Selecting books intelligently is directly linked to how effectively your child can evaluate what he has read. Talking about the best features of a book, the characters and the pictures, gives him a basis for learning these skills. As a more sophisticated reader, he'll distinguish between real and pretend and that the book may be written from one point of view. The events, storyline or even facts, could be represented differently and readers learn to appreciate the author's hand in this.

Developing questioning skills and accepting that books can be criticised as well as valued, takes talking time and effort. Use picture books for older readers, and folk stories or traditional tales if your child is keen. These offer models for making up your own versions, as well as depicting strong characters and moral issues with plenty of talking potential. Encourage your child to gather clues and evidence, to question statements and descriptions. Her previous reading experience will help. If she has read widely she will have a broader foundation from which to anticipate what she will find in other books – in terms of words, structure, organisation and content.

You are not dealing with formal comprehension tasks at this stage. But by discussing ways of comparing and assessing books, you are laying important foundations for later language skills.

Focus on facts: Finding your way around information books

Many factual books for very young children are a lovely introduction to the different ways we can use books. However, they are usually very short and are read in the same way as a story book. The information comes largely from the pictures and from the interesting questions posed in the text. By the junior years, your child will be tackling more complex factual books, and he will learn ways of using them effectively. This takes time as most of his earlier diet has been fiction books which are read from cover to cover.

Project work at school, and group fact-finding missions, will help him approach information books in a different way. He may bring some of this work home or carry over his enthusiasm for a particular theme. Although his teacher will have done her best to provide a range of stimulating books, these have to be shared with other pupils and classes. A visit to your local library should unearth other possibilities.

Knowing where to look

Libraries are daunting places, and warrens of shelves can be very off-putting. Librarians are helpful but busy, so learn how to trace books independently. Together you can grapple with the basics of the classification system, and how to access records. Computer systems may seem terrifying, but remember your computer-literate child is at your side! Once you have the details and have made a note of the codes of interesting titles, show your child how to get to the right shelves. The Dewy system used at most libraries may be similar to that used at school. You'll soon memorise the codes for his latest craze, and make a well-trodden path to the books.

When you have found your patch, browse through the titles, looking for ones he knows from school or picking out those which look attractive. Notice how the classification numbers tie up with the listings you've seen and any titles which are missing that could be ordered. Browse first, noting the format and style of the book, the level of information it offers and its use of technical language. As always, attractive presentation is crucial to hook and hold his interest.

Having the questions so you can look for the answers

Your child will have to learn strategies for using books for a specific purpose. He will move from the vague

'I want to find out more about dinosaurs because I like them . . .'

to the specific

'I want to find out why dinosaurs died out.'

Once you've got hold of a relevant book, examine the contents list and look up key words in the index. Having turned to the relevant chapter your child can then use the sub-headings to narrow down the text even more. Some reference books use different typefaces, boxed information and a question/answer format to hold interest and aid reference skills. (For ways of using factual information refer to page 169.)

Your support now helps make information books more accessible to your child and so offers him a different type of reading experience. It is worth noting that many children, particularly boys, show a strong preference for reading non-fiction books. We accept this in adults, but as a parent you still want to aim for some variety. He may accept a fiction book occasionally, particularly if you track down comic-style formats and short, lively books which grab his attention. Librarians may also be able to recommend fiction titles based on your child's hobbies or interests.

Reading stamina, staying power and big books

The criteria discussed on page 96 are still relevant. You should aim gradually to increase what is termed 'reading stamina'. This is reflected in the length and complexity of books your child feels confident tackling and her ability to complete this reading within a reasonable length of time. Children like to be seen with a 'proper' thick book, and there can be strong peer pressure to keep up. Try to steer your child to realistic choices. It is frustrating if books are too hard too often. The acid test lies in how much your child wants to succeed with a book, and for what reasons.

The content of the books will reflect your child's growing thirst for knowledge, her lively imagination, sense of humour and desire to read about real and difficult issues. Stories based around school, the family and animals can be balanced with fantasy tales and world legends. Reading to your child is a wonderful way of pre-viewing books she might want to read later, or of introducing genres such as poetry. There are useful collections which give a taster of different novels, unlocking doors into fascinating fiction. Some listeners may find the brevity frustrating and unsatisfying, while others are inspired to track down modern classics.

Cover notes

Titles and cover illustrations are carefully researched, but they can be misleading. Some extremists go through a phase when it is taboo to read a book with a picture of a girl on the cover. Older editions of books, and well-thumbed library stock can prevent wonderful titles being touched. Once inside the book, your child may be richly rewarded.

I think the title is off-putting for boys; it sounds babyish. It's an interesting story and wonderfully illustrated. I can recommend it as a good book.

(*Kerry, aged 10, talking about* The Woman Who Went To Fairyland *by Rosalind Kerven, shortlisted for the Children's Book Award*)

Possible trouble spots

By this stage you would expect your child to be on the road to reading confidently and independently. Although there will still be a wide range in abilities and attitudes, you will look for evidence that your child is making her own progress. Carefully voice any concerns you may have with your child's teacher, and develop a joint strategy to help your child. For further details, refer to chapter 11.

A question of attitude

There are three main types of attitude we can identify in early readers. Look down this list and find which category best defines your child:

The confident, mature reader

Lucky you! Your child can't get enough of books, she chooses and reads books constantly and talks eagerly about them. She has favourite authors and styles, but will try new ideas willingly and confidently. She knows she is a good reader and uses her skills to become totally absorbed in silent reading. She uses both school and public libraries regularly and independently.

Don't let her success give you the impression you're not needed. Your involvement and interest will encourage her to read more widely. Talking about her reading deepens her understanding and sophistication. However, do watch that while the books are sufficiently long and demanding, they also match her maturity. Keep up the praise, as your child still needs to know you care and are involved, even though she doesn't show it.

Beth (eight) gives a mature visual response to her reading of *The Suitcase Kid*.

I'll read if I have to or because you want me to

When should we accept that not all children love reading? There's a fine balance between this and neglecting potential for growth and change. Your child can read adequately but appears not to be bothered. He lacks any reading stamina and doesn't offer chances for you to get involved. Constant prodding feels negative and frustrating for both of you.

This attitude is the hardest to analyse and deal with because there are several different causes. Here are a few strategies to try:

- Ease off. Perhaps this is a temporary phase which will only be compounded by any sense of pressure, however well-intentioned.
- Discuss the situation with his teacher. You need to know what he's like in school and work out how to help together.
- Look at what he does read. Is it too boring? Is it too difficult? Does it match his interests? Are there any new avenues he hasn't tried? Might he enjoy a weekly computer magazine or football comic?

> Comic-style books, with strong graphic appeal, are very user friendly. Their speech bubbles and captions are being used a great deal to catch and hold young readers' attention. They may also rehabilitate lost readers; those who have the ability but lack motivation.

(*Retired teacher with wide experience of what makes books popular with children*)

- Examine his general self-confidence and willingness to tackle demanding things. Look at what he does in his spare time. Are you trying to cram too much in?
- Read to him and show genuine satisfaction when you read together. Build upon his strengths and encourage friendships, peer-group interests and hobbies which promote reasons for enjoying reading together.

The struggling reader

Some children will still be finding reading difficult, ranging from those who need the sort of support we would expect to give a real beginner, to those who have problems with a particular strategy or area of reading. Eliminate physical problems as potential causes of your child's reading difficulties by asking for thorough hearing and sight tests. Chapter 11 looks at specific learning difficulties, and helpful organisations are listed in the Appendix on page 217. Like all areas of learning, changes in your child's personal life will affect progress. A move, an emotional crisis or bereavement should be shared with teachers and given time and sensitive consideration. Always start with a visit to the school, seeing the headteacher if you feel your worries aren't being addressed. Try to get concrete information on what extra provision has been made for your child and whether he has been informally assessed.

Ways to help your child

Think carefully about your child's attitude. Does she show boredom or frustration? Is she feeling a failure because reading is compounding rather than relieving her difficulties? Perhaps a radical new approach is called for, with your child being more directly involved. Giving her short, lively but manageable books, with a clear structure, lets you build upon success to give her a new sense of confidence. By now your child will be acutely aware of her lack of progress compared with that of her peers. You and her teacher can help focus on her own progression, offering praise, support and a realistic programme with clear goals.

- Teachers should be able to offer advice about picture books and stories with a simple format which offer challenge and interest to older readers (see the Appendix on page 225).

> ❛ Positive attitudes seem to be achieved when the materials are directly related to his own experiences and sense of humour. ❜

> (*Teacher and parent with three sons*)

- It is even more important that you keep reading to your child, offering variety and interest. Re-read often old favourites which invite your child to participate in a non-threatening way. (Look too at the details below on paired reading.)
- Give him as much pleasurable time sharing useful activities as you can spare.

❝ *He was a slow starter. I played games with him almost daily, writing little stories with common sounds. We played word games, drew pictures, had fun!* ❞

● Find an appreciative audience.

❝ *Asking him to read to his brother gave him a feeling of confidence and superiority which did wonders for his self-esteem.* ❞

● Use television, radio, story-tapes and computer software (see the Appendix on page 233).

● Keep up a regular dialogue with the school and don't feel you are being a pest. Teachers are naturally very busy with many different concerns and priorities. Your child has to be your priority and you won't be happy if your worries are not taken seriously.

● Are your expectations and desires for progress realistic? Your child's attitude, confidence, and willingness to tackle reading, despite its difficulties, should guide your concern.

You should consider seeking outside advice if your child's problems don't appear to be being addressed, and you feel specialist help might be necessary. This process is bound to create considerable stress and tension, but shield your child from this. Organisations which can put you in contact with parents who have coped with similar difficulties or which offer objective, impersonal advice, are well worth contacting.

Whether your struggling reader requires specialist support, a highly structured programme or the freedom to be in control and to select more appropriate books, you will need to be as flexible as possible to meet his needs.

Paired reading

It's difficult to know where to talk about this relatively new technique in shared reading, because it has been applied to a fairly broad range of needs and ages. The basic idea is to offer support by reading the text carefully with your child. The book is selected by your child, and she is in control, setting the pace of your reading by pointing to the words. When she feels confident she will give a sign, possibly by knocking on the table, that she wants to read alone. You should then follow the text carefully, only reading aloud when your child gets stuck on a word. After a short pause to give her time to attempt the word, you should give the word and then start reading again together. Only when your child indicates should you stop and let her continue alone.

The value of this scheme is that your child is in control. She has no sense of failure or negative pressure, and she can dictate the amount of support she feels she needs. It is up to her to set the pace and to decide when she wants to read alone.

To be done properly this technique requires careful training and a consistent, caring approach. As it was originally designed for a parent and child, the approach should offer support to your child whatever her needs. Don't worry if it takes a while to be able to read in harmony and be careful to let your child select appropriate books for effective pairing.

CHAPTER TEN

On the write lines: Writing development

These are exciting years for your budding author, as he starts to use complex skills to experiment and to move, somewhat painfully, above the physical demands of writing. During these years, most children will be able to write in sentences, covering a range of styles and subjects in increasing depth. The problem for parents is in knowing the extent of the tasks which go on in school and in extracting the value of the process which lies behind a completed piece of work. You want signs of progress, but you must relate to other, less visible areas of learning.

Ways of looking at your child's writing

Examining the evidence

Imagine you are given two examples of writing. One is beautifully composed, correctly spelt and perfectly structured; the other tentative, messy, perhaps incomplete and certainly not without errors. Of course the first will delight and the second raise concerns. But how did those words get on the page? If you were told that the first was copied verbatim by the whole class, and the second was a result of complex re-workings and a first response to a new approach, your conclusions might be different.

There has to be a balance when we assess children's writing, and the priority or emphasis of each piece will reflect its function. When you look through your child's work with his teacher or with him, always talk about the ideas and comment upon the positive aspects. Totally perfect pieces may raise as many questions as those with repeated errors. Although progression will not always be clear, you will naturally want evidence that your child is maturing as a writer. The difficulty is in deciding criteria and in accepting that progress can be both gradual and stilted.

A checklist of progress pointers
- content
- maturity of thought
- style
- vocabulary
- length
- presentation
- accuracy
- evidence of variety

This list is not exhaustive, nor does it seek to place relative values on the criteria. It is only a rough yardstick. Being able to make sense of the work is the first task as a reader. Therefore your child's handwriting, punctuation and spelling needs to help achieve this goal if the writing is intended for others. If you are able to read the piece then you can judge the content.

Questions to ask yourself as you read your child's writing

What fresh ideas, angles and styles does it offer? How demanding is the task itself for a youngster emerging from his egocentric origins? What degree of understanding is shown for a particular writing

Horton tower master blaster
Once upon a time there were 4
ninja kids. Rocky, Colt, Funk, and
Tuhtum. One cold misty evening
we collected our torch suits and
trap's. Then we set off to Horton Tower.
But when we got there the door was
locked so we climbed through the
window. "Lets see if there are any
ghosts OK, OK" they replied suddenly
dum de dum dum dum..... Ashkinette
Jumped out he was a dum
de dum dum dum GHOST
Agggthh. We switched on our torch
suits and trap, He disappeared
into the trap. We decided to keep
our torch's on our suits on. As we
walked down the murky tunnel of

a maze (Well that's what it felt
like) all of a sudden I saw
a shiny surface... It was the barrel
of a gun Quick as a whip we
dived down a hole that had live
foxes down it. The foxes **were** Mr
and Mrs fox and three small
fox's. The fox's dug a tunnel to
our house. We kept the fox's as pets.
The End

This entertaining story shows an author confident enough to tease his
audience.

format or genre? For instance, look at an adventure story. How clear and confident is the structure? Does it have a strong start, a logical sequence and a good ending?

What types of words does your child use? Can you see evidence of descriptive skills, of words picked to convey atmosphere or emotion? What words are used to join ideas and sentences? Is there any attempt at dialogue or to break the writing into paragraphs? How long is the writing and how much time did your child have to work on it? Was the work a result of individual effort, or of a shared group activity? How accurate is the spelling and punctuation? Do mistakes follow a clear pattern? What are the main problems and strengths of his writing?

How obvious is a careless mistake?

Do you have any clues about attitude? Are there many careless mistakes? Do you feel the ideas have been carefully thought through? Is there evidence of rapid fatigue and exhaustion, with a sudden and unsatisfactory ending? It is very easy for us to forget how much is going on at each level in writing. When one skill is being developed, concentration on other areas may slip. Our adult writing skills, particularly the stress of having to produce creative, accurate or descriptive prose on demand, are not challenged on a regular basis. Such self-discipline is not easy for anyone, let alone your child who may have newly mastered the physical demands of handwriting and spelling.

If you are anxious

Book a time to visit your child's teacher to look at his work and to discuss the main issues that it raises. If you decide that your concerns are justified and your expectations reasonable, sort out what extra help is available. Consider your child's attitude to writing, as well as any physical difficulties, and get specific hints from the school as to the best support you can offer him at home. Having objectives helps translate concern into positive help rather than anxiety or annoyance. The reasons your child is having problems are very complex:

> *My son has poor fine motor control. He becomes very angry with himself when his hand doesn't produce what his brain requires.*

> *As a little boy, my son loved me to write down stories exactly as he told them. Then he began writing down his own, with some frustration at first. This was overcome by being able to tell stories onto a tape.*

> *He is left-handed and he still finds writing a trial.*

The physical demands of writing cause frustration to many children. If you can find other ways of recording your child's ideas, you are still helping his writing and self-confidence. *Jurassic Park*, the fastest selling book last year, is unlikely to have been written by hand! Balance activities to firm up physical skills with those which focus on creative powers.

> *I sit with him, so he can bounce ideas off me. I encourage him to get the work done instead of staring into space, which is the main problem.*

Concentration is central to writing, and an elusive quality, particularly with so many lively interests which fill your child's time. I can wax lyrical about shared enjoyment, but at the hard end, it feels anything but! As your child approaches secondary school, he'll need study skills and self-discipline so that his homework isn't usually copied on the bus to school. Teachers require your support and knowledge of your child's interests to make at least some writing tolerable.

Pressure or encouragement

There is a slim but crucial difference between these two approaches, so how do you ensure you are helping rather than hindering? The golden rule is 'Know your child and if it works happily for him, do it!'

> *I kept it fun so he enjoyed doing it and thought of it as special time together.*

Parents put pressure on their children if they have unrealistic expectations. Perhaps you found writing and learning spellings particularly easy, or have an older child with a language gift. If your child is a fluent, confident reader it can also be harder to accept that she doesn't respond as keenly to written work. We expect a direct link between avid readers and good spellers, but this doesn't always hold true.

Your expectations will also be coloured by what your child's peers seem capable of. Comparison with others serves no value unless it highlights your child's particular needs rather than her failures. Don't add to your child's difficulties by looking for results too quickly, but work out step-by-step objectives to help her.

Your support will give your child the confidence to keep trying; your pressure could lead him to clam up with an overwhelming fear of failure.

> *I know this isn't your best!*

> *Your sister writes to beautifully . . .*

> *If you are were careful, and concentrated, you wouldn't make all these mistakes.*

Watch how you phrase things: it's so easy to cause emotional stress by implying that your child has let you down, possibly through lack of effort. Yes, there are children who respond to firm encouragement, but this is very different from rejecting work because it doesn't measure up. We can't always produce our best.

Refer back to the quality of work you know he can achieve.

Offer real and interesting motives for writing, but respect that he won't always be in the mood. Your child should know that you care, that you are proud of his achievements and want to help him overcome problems. Encouragement is about building upon your shared strengths and creating an atmosphere of trust and respect. You can't force your way in if your child refuses to co-operate. This can be both frustrating and hurtful, and can only be overcome by consistent and sensitive handling.

Keep your work together short and regular, if and when your child does show an interest. As far as possible steer him towards writing activities he will find manageable as well as enjoyable. Rather like shared reading, if you are able to offer as much support as he needs to achieve his goal, you can avoid encouragement tipping over into negative pressure.

What types of writing go on in school?

There is of course, an enormous variety of writing activities.

Many children have a book for creative writing and a personal diary for recording special events and private thoughts. They may also have exercise books for handwriting and more structured class work – often related to learning spelling or grammar rules – together with simple comprehension work linked to class reading. Writing features strongly in other curriculum areas, for example in recording results of science and technology experiments, researching information for project work and jotting down maths problem-solving tasks.

There will be examples of more poetic writing, often inspired by a framework given to the whole class such as working on riddles or similes. Your child might enjoy inventing lyrics for his favourite tunes and using class time to follow creative interests of his own.

Look on the class library shelves for school-made books, often

PART 4: ON THE WRITE LINES: WRITING DEVELOPMENT

SPACE

```
Everything starts off in the middle of space.
Mist and dust pour out
And form rocks and figures.
A rocket plunges
To infinity
Like a bottle in distress.
The moon is dead
Bus aliens would be flying around
Out there
Somewhere!
```

                    Neil Langholz

MY DREAM IN SPACE

I flew through space in my rocket
I went so fast I couldn't stop it.
I hit the moon and bounced off Mars,
Flew round Pluto straight up to the stars.
I turned sharp right and came straight down
And landed in my dressing gown.

Francesca Andreoli 6Bm
Prizewinner

WHAT AM I?

Beautiful, bold and bright
Utterly unique.
Twisting, twirling torso.
Twinkling, tranquil togetherness.
Elegant European emblem.
Rare and rewarding.
Fluttering, flying fantasy.
• Larvae like leaves Lipidoptera
Young, yellow and yearly.

Elaine Sherred 5Jn

These accomplished poems and riddles took plenty of talking and many messy drafts to reach this quality.

the result of collaborative writing, either by the whole class responding to a common theme, or by groups sharing their skills to develop a book they can all feel proud of. You may not see tangible evidence of your child's involvement on every page. However, he will have learnt a great deal about the social side of writing, of brainstorming sessions, developing ideas and then drafting and redrafting until all are satisfied with their published work. The illustrations, shape, style and presentation of the book are all a crucial part of the work.

HELP YOUR CHILD WITH READING AND WRITING

in the round house it was very warm Because the wind blows
Soth most of the time. and there is a nice warm fire. and it
is very dark even with out doors with doors on it will
be very dark. it was very smely because there was
a fire and the smoke was smelly. and there was
a chimminy so but as there was a chimminy the smoke
was hot but as there was a chimminy the smoke
and the sparks would go up and out it wold rise to the top very sinely
the round house can get in bute they were but hexagon so it would not seal in
is it did go on fire it would go up in 30 miuts we where siting round the fire
on hay but on in of the hay was animal skins like Sheep scins.
the wall where made of wevled sticks and they Put a mixer of mud cow dung
and animel hear. the round was very dry in side. it wold not be dry if ther
was a chimminy because the rain would get in dry side mudy wird siuppy
and the rain would put the rise out. at narvest they made a dumy out of
straw so the spirit would go in side it wen harvest had finsh they chuck it out
So the Spirit should go in to the seeds. the round was so put in disarter. it was mudy in
the andvent.

Well remembered ouiver!

Anglo - saxons

Saxons came from germany
after about 400.ad. They
~~settet~~ settled down and
married english people and
became anglo-saxons. They
liked bright coloured
clothes made from wool
cotton and leather. They
vere   cleuer   with
gold   and   made
ntric   ate peices   of
ewell   ery using   precious
ones   especia   lly rubies
from   abroad.

A group of eight-year-olds researched and then responded to their own
interests for a history project.

How can I help at home?

Home learning schemes – can they work for your child?

You must assess this for yourself by getting your little monster to choose and test-drive with you. (Refer back to page 861 and to the Appendix on page 220 for details about how to choose workbooks.) Many less confident writers get great satisfaction from filling in, adding sentences and completing boxes, with an even bigger glow of pride when they sense they have got the right answers. Even if he doesn't learn what you expect him to, concentration, self-discipline and confidence improve for some. Try another tac if he's not enjoying it. These studies shouldn't take the place of more real and risky forms of writing in which he actually has to create things for himself.

'How do I get him started? I can't just tell him to write a story'

Writing is a messy and lively activity, not a form of solitary confinement to be threatened when you reach exasperation point with your kids quarrelling over the lego. Talk provides the angles for getting your child keen to write, and the ammunition, or word-power, he needs to do this successfully. Functional writing, like a message for the babysitter, letters or describing a mystery object, is easy to get going. Copying crosswords and quiz ideas is useful as a springboard to making up your own. The more discussion you have had, the more thorough and clearly thought out your child's writing is likely to be.

Use stories, fables and poems as a model for creative writing as this eases your child into the more risky area of creative and imaginative work. With creative writing, children often lack a sense of purpose. Providing a framework helps give direction. Poems and fables, for example, may contain messages; they have clear formats,

HELP YOUR CHILD WITH READING AND WRITING

Beth Lindsay

Anger

Anger is red and orange.

The taste of anger is hot water and steam.

Anger smells of sizzling spaghetti

It Looks Like a big fire on a massive building

Anger sounds Like tigers roaring.

It feels it burning and sweaty

Nicola

Ashamed is the Colour dark dark blue.

It taste like Sour milk.

The smell is like Pickled Onions

Rain falling on a cold day thats what it looks like.

Sounding like a cat meowing in the dark.

feels like cold water

These eight-year-olds used their senses to describe some strong emotions.

PART 4: ON THE WRITE LINES: WRITING DEVELOPMENT

and are not dauntingly long. Try taking a favourite fable as a model and asking your child to rewrite it – or, even better, to write her own fable giving the same message.

<u>Old mans Beard</u>

One day in the month of October in a far off village in India there lived a man called Ragive. Ragive was very poor and he went out to collect berries to eat.

The best berries were always the hardest to find. Ragive saw some in among a very prickly thorn bush. So he bent down to get the ~~down in get~~ berries and got caught up. He pulled but he couldn't get free. It began to get dark. Ragive could hear the wolves howling. He was scared. The sound got nearer. He pulled himself away and left his long white beard in the thorn Bush. He was safe. Every October certain bushes are ~~covered~~ Covered with these white fluff. I wonder if its Ragives beard?   Excellent Elliott

Elliott has obviously read widely and thought through his ideas for this fable telling how a plant got its name.

Notice together the qualities you enjoy in good fiction and poetry: careful sequencing and control, powerful characterisation, humour, vivid descriptions and astute observations. Help him gain a sense of pacing and confidence in his role as a writer.

Say your child comes to you with a vague idea about writing a story about firework night. Start by assessing where her main interest lies and how she wants the story to develop. Collect lots of descriptive, lively sound words and try to relive the excitement of the sounds, sight and smell of fireworks, the warmth of the bonfire, etc. You could jot down key words and ideas together. Then talk about how her story could begin, what characters are involved and what action takes place.

<u>My friendly dragon</u>

There was a whizz a bang and pop and a few stars then a dragon popped out of a fire work.
He had a grey chest with green legs and great big eyes all fat and bulgy his tumy was fat. He had purple hairs and a long tongue. He had long bumpy spikes on his back, his feet were webbed with claws. He came in the house and had some supper and slept the night. In the morning we picked Sammy up and she was not afraid because she had a dragon of her own. We played in the ash from the bonfire. We got very messy it was really fun then we all got in the bath together. Bubble! bubble! Then we played in the bath and Sammy stayed the night. In the morning we went to the cinema and then when we came home we played then we had lunch then went to the park. It was fun, we got an ice-cream then Sammy went home.

By Francesca

Francesca is already experimenting with descriptive detail and humour.

Staying power?

As with their reading, children of this age are developing a writing stamina which demands a great deal of concentration and physical control. Ideas tumble out in a chaotic rush, and your child then has to create some order and focus. Like any demanding task, the rewards come when you have the satisfaction of having completed something worthwhile and valued. Talking together is the best way of drawing out your child's skills and letting her achieve this. Of course there will be times when a great idea lasts a few lines before being dropped in the bin, but she is the author and rejects are very much part of the business. Feedback is vital to your child's willingness to write and you must show her you care through offering constructive advice.

Bright ideas for less confident writers

- Write a story for a little brother, sister or convenient toddler neighbour. Involving this live audience while enjoying the status of being the expert has made this approach a success in schools. It offers the perfect excuse to re-read favourite picture books as part of your research, as you'll need ideas for what theme and presentation would suit your toddler. The other great value of writing a picture book is that the text has to be kept clear, short and simple. The illustrations, pop-out or lift-the-flap designs become an integral part of the work. You also have the real audience on hand to share in the success and to evaluate your book.

- Use the local newspaper as a source about topical issues. Perhaps your child could write in with ideas about improving playground facilities, or with suggestions for a safe cycle track.

- Write jokes and riddles for family and friends to quiz over.

- Write a play with friends, possibly based on a favourite book or television programme.

- Research places of interest when your family books a holiday, writing letters for more information or special offers. Once on holiday keep a diary and evaluate the attractions, seeing how they measured up to expectations.

HELP YOUR CHILD WITH READING AND WRITING

- Spells for Halloween, recipes for Christmas and Pancake day, all combine writing with a special family occasion.

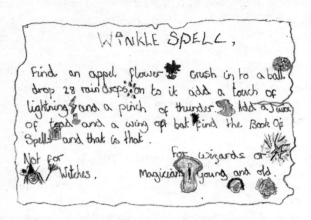

This extract from Natalie's story includes a winkle spell!

- Produce personal ABCs to match your child's interests, from Disney characters to types of cars.
- If you want a simple structure to writing, offer your child a model such as

    'If I had a . . . , I would . . .'
    'One, two, How do you do?/Three, four . . .'
    'On misty Monday morning we . . ./On terrible Tuesday tea-time we . . .'
    'Red is for danger, lights blaring bright, red are my pyjamas I wear in the night . . .'

- Cover versions of favourite stories allow some copying, whilst requiring a few original sentences.
- Annotate a picture, map, puzzle or maze for a friend to solve.
- Cut out pictures of people from comics and magazines and invent a criminal record file for them!

Other ways of helping

'His spelling is awful! What can I do to help?'

Use the same approaches outlined in chapter 6, or adapt the more advanced ideas given on pages 198–201. When you come to edit work together, ask your child to read it aloud, as this could draw her attention to careless errors. When giving her words that she needs, write them down rather than dictating the letters and use the 'look, say, cover, write and check' technique (see page 74) later on selected words.

Silly sentences help remember knotting strings of letters, such as 'I caught my daughter who was feeling fraught so we drowned our sorrows with laughter'. Collect groups of words even when the sound patterns are different as you are focusing on the visual pattern too.

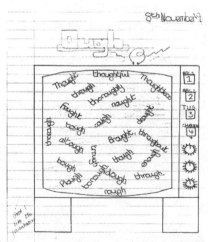

Ian shows an interesting way of presenting '-ough' spellings.

Help your child with alphabet and dictionary skills, showing her ways to remember the order, and breaking down the dictionary into manageable chunks. Look at what letter is halfway through your dictionary, what letter comes a quarter of the way through, etc. and make up a silly sentence using words starting with each of these letters. Set her humorous challenges through which she can use and explore her dictionary.

Handwriting.

Again, refer back to chapter 6. If you are worried about presentation always ask the school how you can help. Copying out favourite poems for a personal anthology, or a draft letter into a final copy may offer more satisfaction than exercises repeating one letter. The teacher will be able to suggest ways of tailoring work to reach your child's particular problem.

As with learning spellings, it helps to practise writing whole words which contain a similar flow of letters, to get the feel of writing consistently.

Presentation is also about the sizing of letters, spacing, conformity and minimal blotches and crossing out. Having a genuine pride in her work, because it is being read for a purpose, will raise her efforts. You and your child's teacher appreciate the sweat behind the lines, even when the end result is far from perfect.

CHAPTER ELEVEN

Children with special language needs

It is vital that we address the educational needs of the one in five children who require some form of special attention. They have just as much a right to enjoy the pleasures of literacy as other children. Yet funding is tight, which puts pressure on the way children with special needs can be catered for within the National Curriculum. Because the range of problems is so vast, how they are discovered and treated varies enormously. By the time your child is seven you would expect any difficulties to be fairly clear, resulting in expert diagnosis and support being made available. Realistically, there are many reasons why this is not always the case.

Teachers are generally very busy, caring professionals. Although trained to look for potential problems they can lack expertise about specific difficulties. They are fully occupied with a class load of different capabilities, personalities, behaviours and backgrounds. Yet all their pupils must be served a wide and ambitious curriculum diet. The symptoms children show may be similar, but their causes quite different. Unless the teacher has a wide experience of learning difficulties, diagnosis could be delayed.

Parents sometimes complain that teachers are dismissive or defensive when they raise doubts about their child's progress. If you have regular and positive communication with the school, this is less likely to happen. The emphasis is not on doubting the teacher's capabilities, but upon ensuring that your child's needs are addressed. If you are told that boys take longer to acquire language skills, that there are children who are far slower or that your child is making steady progress but will probably soon take-off, this could well be true. The teacher is not being dismissive, but she cannot know your child as well as you do. Equally, your natural concern for your child's progress can distort the true picture. Objectivity and balance are called for and this is best achieved through working out a realistic timetable for assessment with the school. To achieve this requires a superhuman blend of realism, honesty, patience and persistence.

A real problem, or just developing at her own rate?

Earlier chapters have focused on the need to allow your child to progress naturally at her own pace by fending off over-anxiety and pressure. But if your child does have a problem the sooner she receives expert help, the better. You have a unique understanding of your own child's emotional, mental and physical development. You must therefore be centre-stage when it comes to deciding whether there could be a problem. Good communication with the school is then essential to establish the nature of your child's difficulties.

If the problem is one of attitude or concentration, informal chats should allow you and the teacher jointly to work out a programme, ranging from giving her gentle support to more tenacious and regular prompting. In the same way, if your child's reading strategies are inefficient, a plan of action can be drawn up to help her. Perhaps she relies too much on sounding out words or she glosses over the story and doesn't pay enough attention to the details on the page. Both cases can be resolved by appropriate support. In writing too, specific problems such as repeatedly reversing letters, confusing spellings or poor organisation can all be treated. But what if these are themselves symptoms of more complex difficulties, requiring specialist and long-term support to correct?

A methodical analysis of the list below will help you decide whether your child's problems warrant further investigation.

Firstly consider physical details:

1   When did your child learn to talk, and walk? Has there been a general delay in development, or are language problems related to speech difficulties?
2   Have you checked his sight? Watch him as he reads. How does he scan the page? Does he screw up his eyes, squint, rub his eyes or keep moving the book around? What about balance and headaches? These signs should be discussed with your doctor. Myopia (short-sightedness), hypermetropia (long-sightedness) and astigmatisms all cause blurring and distortions for which your child learns to compensate. The class environment, the crowded playground and small print texts bring previously buried problems to light. Help by enhancing her listening skills, her sense of rhythm and use of non-visual clues. Give her books which have short lines, good spacing and large but not thick print.

❛ *The letters jump around and won't let me read them.* ❜

For some children reading is a nightmare because the words will not stay still, or they are seen through a fog. Possible solutions range from using coloured glasses, or reflexology treatment, to a careful eye test and a skilled optician finding glasses to relieve the problem. One girl struggled with this difficulty undetected until she was ten. She'd looked at her friend's book, found that her words were jumping around too, so assumed it to be the norm. Unless we ask such children what they actually see on the page, even a standard school eye test may not detect their problem. (Both eyes should be tested together as it is here that the difficulty may occur.) See the Appendix on page 217 for further advice.

3   Can he hear well? This may relate back to how and when he learnt to speak, his social behaviour and ability to follow instructions independently. When hearing loss is related to middle ear infections it is erratic and open to misinterpretation. The symptoms 'poor attention', 'a dreamer', 'so forgetful' hold true for the child with weak concentration too. A child with some hearing loss will often withdraw from group discussions, or offer his opinion very loudly and frequently. Again, these actions can have a number of causes. Add to this temper outbursts, frustration and attention-seeking behaviour, and the problems of diagnosis multiply!

A thorough hearing test removes some doubt although erratic hearing loss is difficult to detect. If you discover your child has a slight loss, make sure staff know, and look for books with strong visual appeal to aid his reading. Bright novelty books and those with detailed illustrations both add interest and give a basis for discussing the story. Talking time is even more important where delayed diagnosis has resulted in your child having a limited language experience.

4   Is she particularly clumsy, with weak fine-motor skills? The Dyspraxia Trust should be able to provide advice and support. (See the Appendix on page 218 and page 82).

5   Has your child missed schooling?

6   Have there been recent changes which have resulted in emotional upset for your child? Share necessary information with the school to help your child.

Dyslexia, still a knotty problem

This term is given to a specific learning difficulty which can affect reading, writing and spelling, but which has an impact on the whole of your child's way of life. It is three times more common in boys, and is often hereditary. It is estimated to affect up to ten per cent of the population with around four per cent of these cases being severe enough to require support throughout their education. A staggering three children in every class will have some degree of difficulty. If your child shows all or several of the following symptoms you should seek further advice:

1 He has problems with orientation, from tying shoe laces to following directions.
2 He finds it hard to put things in sequence, was slow to learn the days of the week, or (for older children) to tell the time. He can't copy patterns using coloured beads or construction blocks.
3 He was late deciding whether to use his left or right hand for writing, or is cross-lateral (see page 82).
4 He is generally clumsy and poorly co-ordinated.
5 He has a weak short-term memory. He can't take phone messages, remember things for school or complete a sequence of three instructions accurately. When reading, he remembers a word, then forgets it when reading a few lines below.
6 His speech was delayed for no physical reason. He also has poor listening skills and powers of observation.
7 He experiences particular difficulty with reading or spelling.
8 He reverses letters, figures and even whole words.
9 He shows poor concentration when reading and writing.
10 Is he otherwise bright and responsive?
11 Do other members of the family show similar problems?

You need a more detailed list related to the age of your child for a full picture. For example, a child over nine might be expected to remember mathematical tables, music symbols and more complex spellings. A pre-school child's symptoms will be confined to speech difficulties, an inability to label objects, co-ordination problems and the muddling of simple concepts like up and down. Seek expert advice if you have any doubts.

Getting help

1 Talk to the class teacher early in the school year to allow adequate time to monitor the situation.
2 By the middle term you can then ask to discuss assessment with the headteacher.
3 Back up any request for referral to outside bodies (such as Language and Numeracy Support Services (LANSS) or Special Educational Needs Support Services (SENSS)) in writing.
4 Make an appointment, via the school if possible, for a LEA psychologist to visit. Your child may be observed in class and have a formal assessment later. Slight problems can be dealt with by the class teacher having additional support from the Special Needs Support Services. You should have a written report detailing these arrangements. Your child's progress will then be reviewed again within a year.
5 However, it may be necessary to call upon other professionals so that a statement of your child's needs can be made. Severe difficulties require full-time teaching at a special unit or school.
6 Whatever the outcome of any assessment, national and regional organisations are invaluable for support and practical advice (see the Appendix on page 217).

Other routes to assessment

7 Alternatively, talk to your health visitor, doctor or Community Medical Officer and try to arrange an assessment through a local centre or hospital.

8 Organisations such as the Dyslexia Institute can arrange for a thorough, but expensive, independent assessment.

Recent changes in the Code of Practice covering assessment aim to ensure that all special educational needs are identified and assessed as early and as quickly (but thoroughly) as possible. The procedure follows five stages, the first three being dealt with in school, the final two stages involving outside agencies. Local support groups help interpret how the rules fit your case. Their expertise is useful in guiding letters through a fog of red tape, jargon and legislation so that they actually reach their intended target and you get results.

How can I help at home?

All children get tired after school but your child may be exhausted. At worst, school becomes an ordeal, compounded by lack of self-esteem and sheer frustration. Home is a safe haven so leave remedial work alone and help him enjoy himself.

- Give him a wide experience and plenty of talking time to increase his general knowledge and develop personal interests. Frequent visits to interesting places and walks are ideal but they take time to organise and execute.

- Books! Dyslexia children still love books, so visit your library often. Read to him as much as he'll allow from a wide range of books. Use tapes and other media to boost a love of literature and an interest in hobbies. Listen to him read every day using entertaining books and a positive approach.

- Find special resources and games to tackle your child's specific needs. Memory games are particularly relevant, as are simple word games.
- Feel positive, find hobbies he's good at. Help keep up that purposeful, active spirit which is so crucial in overcoming learning difficulties.
- Relax together. The tensions you feel will undoubtedly be reflected in the stress and anxiety shouldered by your child. Find ways of channelling strong emotions and make time to talk through his problems. Watch television and play with construction models.
- Help him to be independent. He needs your help to get organised and to perform tasks like dressing, telling the time and following instructions. Practise these essential life-skills but avoid failure by keeping your goals simple and realistic.

Teaching methods are multi-sensory, that is they use a variety of approaches to overcome problems. Talking, listening, seeing and even touching are all part of the process. Your child's programme may involve an intensive and highly organised approach to letter/sound relations, syllables, spelling rules and language structure. Your child may want help at home to practise skills so do keep informed through regular contact with his teachers.

A list of don'ts!

These are ideal aims. No one will pretend that the stress and anxiety you feel is easy to contain.

- Don't try to force or prolong activities when there are clear signs that your child has had enough. Resist the feeling that, if she only tried a bit more or worked harder, her troubles would be over. When encouragement tips over into pressure, the results are rarely successful.
- Don't let your anxiety show, but try to talk positively about how you can work together.

- Don't expect sudden results. Progress may be slow, but assure your child that it's there.

Listening to adults who have experienced language learning difficulties is a telling way of assessing the strains and feelings of inadequacy your child may endure.

> ❝ I will say to my kids – make sure you learn to read and write; you don't want to be a no-hoper thicko like me. ❞
>
> (A young adult male)

> ❝ She keeps saying 'Mummy read me a story' and I have to keep making excuses, it's awful. ❞

> ❝ I didn't read for pleasure until in my twenties. This has made me more committed to encourage my own children to enjoy all aspects of reading and writing. ❞

Your child may be locked in a world of frustrations and disappointments. He is repeatedly urged to try harder when the tasks he face already demand maximum effort. Don't let him use his difficulties as an excuse, yet shield him from the failures he is bound to encounter. A positive, loving and active response to his problems will cushion the blows and give him a pride in what he can do to balance the fears of what he can't.

Bilingualism

Until recently children were discouraged from using their native tongue if it wasn't English, as it was felt that grappling with two or more languages would be too demanding. In fact, confident self-expression in one language helps when learning another. There is now a far greater concern to respect and strengthen mother tongue skills. After all, there are many close communities where a child rarely needs to talk English outside school, and her language is of course part of her cultural identity.

There are tremendous challenges facing children who have to learn a new language when they start school, with all the cultural and structural rules that are part and parcel of the words and sentences. Teachers work hard to find some common ground and interests so as to establish a sense of trust. Learners must be willing to take risks and must be driven by a strong sense of purpose; this is particularly true of second language learners.

> ghosts   Ghosts
>
> Ghosts look like sheets with th
>
> holes in them. The holes
>
> are for the eyes. The ghosts
>
> make scary noises.

> charles dickens
>
> Born 1812. He was the second of 8 childre.
> father, Jhon dickens in the nave pay office.
> apter loosing job, moved to London. No many
> forst in to debtor's prision, most of family in
> prison with father, charle, now twelve
> cherles working in blacking pactory for one
> shilling (5p) a day spehonce very bad wood not
> food but that.

These contrasting samples from second language learners reflect different needs to learn English. The first girl is from a close community where no English is spoken at all outside school. The second girl reached an impressive standard in a year due to sheer determination to make herself understood.

PART 4: CHILDREN WITH SPECIAL LANGUAGE NEEDS

Your bilingual child must find ways of joining in with the rest of the class. Teachers carefully monitor your child's progress as she moves from watching, to using non-verbal communication to labelling with single words. If no one in the school speaks your child's language, this is the main way she will learn to communicate. Specialist teachers provide essential back-up and some withdrawal time from the strains of the classroom. They help your child develop language skills by focusing upon her known interests and experience so she communicates confidently. Some schools find a buddy system useful, whereby your child is paired with another (but different) second language learner who can appreciate the stresses she faces.

Feel confident that any positive home support is useful regardless of how well you speak English. Even where there is no adult who can understand your child reading English, the attention and bond through sharing books remains crucial. Borrow dual language books from the school and library to enable shared discussion, but listen to your child read other English books too. Reading and writing activities in your own language will be refining skills which she can later transfer to her expression in English. The goals of comprehension, quality writing and mature study skills remain the same.

I've heard about a Reading Recovery Programme. What is it, and how does it work?

This scheme targets children who are having problems from a very early stage and gives them intensive support so they can recover lost ground. It was devised by Dame Marie Clay in New Zealand and was first used here in 1990. The aim is to offer daily sessions to six-year-olds who lag behind in reading progress. This gives children a boost and reduces the stigma of failure before it takes hold.

The publicity surrounding this approach is due partly to political considerations and partly to the costs of funding such a programme. Yet early results have been very promising, with a 98 per cent success rate reported by Surrey in the first few years of its introduction there. As in other schemes, parental support is central to its success.

Each programme is tailored to individual needs and requires a specially-trained teacher. The work is challenging and intensive for both child and teacher and involves a variety of activities in each session. A half-hour's tuition might include:

- re-reading familiar books, focusing on accuracy;
- a shared writing activity, perhaps cutting up the sentences and re-building the story again;
- practice in letter, sound and word analysis including using magnetic letters and matching games;
- focusing on sounds within words when reading and writing, and looking at regular patterns;
- listening skills, so that children can clearly hear different sound patterns;
- reading together, preparing a new book for the next sessions.

Contact your local school or education authority to find out if a similar scheme operates in your area.

Gifted children

Very able readers also have special educational needs which are difficult to meet within a busy classroom. If your child is reading confidently before school, make sure you explain this to her teacher. Discuss ways of locating suitable books, adapting reading schemes and charting out an individual programme. You want your child to enjoy her skills and to be challenged by new demands, whilst allowing her plenty of time to consolidate her learning.

❝ *'I'm not a dog!'* ❞

This was how some friends discovered that their three-year-old was a reader! Her father, when passing a written notice barring dogs from the grounds of a stately home, jokingly said that his daughter wasn't allowed in.

Once their daughter started school, they had to battle to prevent her being put through a set reading scheme. Both teacher, parents and child had to work out a strategy which let the girl enjoy a happy, sharing and stretching role within the class. (See the Appendix on pages 218–219 for sources of advice.) Your child's confidence in writing may take a different pattern as her knowledge through reading gives her a strong sense of what is 'right'. This can make her less willing to take risks and experiment. If this is the case, ask her teacher to give practical hints on how to increase her confidence in exploring new areas of learning.

CHAPTER TWELVE

Moving out: Reading independently

Perhaps you feel redundant in these final years at primary school. Your child will be reading to herself and no longer seems to need or want your support. She may be off school reading schemes, left to roam and select books freely. Time to back off and get on with the gardening? Or time to find out what's being recommended and encouraged at school so you can share books pleasurably in new ways?

I'm still here!

Show her that you respect her independence, but that you value time sharing books and that you are always willing to learn about what she's reading. Choosing and buying books together is something you can do: your purse-power is still important! Visit jumble sales, car boot sales and second-hand shops, or organise a book-swap, to make your money go further. The necessity of driving her to the library can be a blessing in disguise. You may go off to different shelves, but you have the chance to talk about selections together. Membership of clubs and organisations is another useful strategy to keep in touch and share information.

PART 5: MOVING OUT: READING INDEPENDENTLY

❝ *What are we aiming for, and how do I know my child is really fluent?* ❞

If she doesn't want to read to you any more encourage her to discuss what she's reading critically, and to offer examples from the text. Your genuine interest and tact will ensure this doesn't feel like an inquisition! Look at your child absorbed with a book. Does she read swiftly yet also manage to be deeply engrossed in the story? A fluent reader combines rapid reading with a personal involvement. Mature readers should adapt their style and pace to suit different purposes, reading meticulously when the occasion demands. So do bring home the message that speed isn't everything when it comes to measuring fluency.

When she does read aloud notice her confidence and control. Does she read with good expression, not losing the thread of the meaning when she comes to an unfamiliar word? How does she cope with such words, and what level of accuracy does she show? Does she notice and try to correct errors, and do these mistakes usually show the same weakness? Does she understand the subtleties of the text, looking beneath the surface for a deeper meaning? How does she choose fiction? Is she willing to take up new and challenging reading and to vary her diet?

Even the able need help

A fluent reader doesn't necessarily have the maturity to cope with all she's reading. Odd words escape us all as we focus on the storyline and complex characters, and sub-plots need talking through. Ideally she'll ask when pieces of the jigsaw don't seem to fit, but let her know you welcome such questions. Encourage her to use all the clues to get the full value from a book. Techniques such as skimming, scanning and interrogating the text help her comprehension skills. Yet reading for pleasure should still take pride of place:

❝ *Family reading sessions are great at any age,
providing everyone is enjoying what's on offer . . .
sharing a book is very special.* **❞**

(Teacher)

You may be lucky enough to get a personal invite to share in your child's reading revels:

❝ *I read this book first then I asked my Mum to read
it for me because I wanted to listen to it again and
because I thought it was excellent!* **❞**

(Paul, 10, talking about Gulf by Robert Westall)

How do we distinguish and help poorer readers at eleven?

Whatever your child's abilities, a prime objective is to keep him reading. Poorer readers still focus much of their attention on decoding, actually making sense of the words. If reading is too much effort, is erratic and infrequent, he's likely to switch off. He needs your support and interest to nurture a will to succeed.

But there are plenty of books on the shelf!

It takes more than availability to tempt an unwilling child into regular reading habits. Encourage him to choose for himself, but guide him so that his reading stamina is built up gradually. Longer books are intimidating yet he doesn't want 'baby' titles. Humour, picture books, books with a personal interest and media tie-ins all help as long as they roughly match his reading ability. There are no hard and fast rules though. If he's drawn to an epic, make sure he succeeds by offering to share the reading adventure together.

❝ *It was my longest read ever and my Mum felt it was so long-winded I'd never finish it. But it wasn't and I did!* ❞

(*Michael talking about the 390 page wonders of* Salamandastron
by Brian Jacques)

When the writing is gripping, it's amazing what your child can achieve:

❝ *I'm not usually a strong reader, my brother is. But I got stuck into the adventure and my mind ran riot in the feasts and the battles. It was all so real and exciting and such a challenge to finish!* ❞

(*David, talking about the same book*)

Poorer readers find it hard focusing on detail: they miss points and are easily confused. Is this due to poor attention, lack of accuracy or disinterest? Assess the root causes so he gets appropriate support. His confidence is very fragile, but plenty of talking time, word games and help with reading clues should bring positive results. Weaker readers often lack a broad reading background and a wider vocabulary. Their experience of story structures may be limited. All these factors combine to produce the face value reading just described. Pick stories with strong contrasts and bold characters which help his interpretation skills.

'Real' reading makes demands but your child needs to stick with it for long enough to appreciate that it also brings rich rewards.

Enjoying fiction

Selecting fiction

Picture books . . . still?

Whatever the ability of your child, don't neglect picture books. The

Principal of a wonderful Resource Centre describes how eleven-year-olds reacted to the introduction of quality picture books:

> ❮ *In this case my excitement for the books was matched by the pupils' enthusiasm. From the most able to the least able readers, they devoured the books. Sitting in groups at small tables, they passed the books around and told each other about them.* ❯

Ask the kids

Children are discerning. Yes, they might be drawn into fads, whether related to other media, or prompted by a basic instinct (do the horror crazes fit this category?!). Yet classic fiction survives the tests of time, and children can respond to a wide range of writers. However, they show considerable brand loyalty when selecting fiction. Even at 11, three authors usually top the charts:

- Roald Dahl 'a clear winner right across the ability range' (survey results, teacher). Children like his wicked 'rude' humour, and his 'playful, merry style' (Ian, aged 9). The author himself acknowledged that his readers aren't fooled by the nastiness of some of the happenings: 'They're fun, and things that wouldn't really happen in real life' (Jonathan, aged 11).
- Enid Blyton is enjoyed for her spirit of adventure. She is like a reassuring habit which even older readers are reluctant to break because her books have a relaxing familiarity. Younger children like her because 'she has thick books' (Helen, aged 7).
- Dick King-Smith is widely regarded because of his ability to captivate through his vivid animal characters and humour.

Children enjoy an element of suspense, being gripped by sheer panic. They go for books which encourage empathy yet which reach out to new horizons. Many, such as Tanya, aged 9 '. . . like stories that are funny, adventurous and have a happy ending'.

Children are both astute and lively in how they respond to good books, as these extracts clearly show (some of which are kindly loaned by organisers of the Children's Book Award):

> *It's lovely, and I like the snowman saying NEVERWOZANOCEROS.*
>
> (Alison, 4, about Penguin Small *by Mick Inkpen*)

> *I laughed and laughed. So did my brother.*
>
> (Jonathan, 5, about Dilly and the Pirates *by Tony Bradman*)

> *They nearly make me cry. The colours are beautiful.*
>
> (Zoe, 7, about the illustrations in Snowy *by Berlie Doherty and illustrated by Keith Brown*)

> *Anyone who is unhappy at school should read this book – their troubles will soon be over!*
>
> (Neil, 9, about The Angel of Nithill Road *by Anne Fine*)

> *Super Cool! Best story I've ever heard!*

> *I loved this book because it was so wittily written, but with a great deal of understanding worked in. It could help children cope with situations like it.*
>
> (Metan, 9, and Polly, 11, of The Suitcase Kid *by Jacqueline Wilson*)

> *The descriptive writing made this story come alive for me. I could picture it clearly in my mind. It was a very good read, but I wish they could have met up with their mother once again!*
>
> (Lindsey, 11, of The Wheel of Surya *by Jamila Gavin*)

The sophistication and understanding evident in these comments is a testimony to the maturity to which young readers can aspire.

HELP YOUR CHILD WITH READING AND WRITING

GULF

I never relized how young people
were when they joined the army.
It made pictures out of words for me
and seemed real. I can really see the
pillows as sand bags. I watched
with Tom in astonishment and horror!
and at the end of the book I hated
the Americans! It took a while for
me to relized Andy was tellepathic
but when I did I understood
all that happened

By Jessica Thomas
(age 11)

The Suitcase
Kid

This book explains the difficulty of divorce and how the child takes it all in
very well. I liked the book because of the detail of the text and the reality which
had gone in to the books.
The personalities of the characters were superb and I also liked the way
Andy treasured Radish.

Clare Duffy
age 10.

Other bright ideas for ways of responding to fiction books

Apart from talking and sharing your interpretations, try some more
unusual ways of working with fiction.

- Instead of getting your child to analyse a character, ask her
  to imagine how that character would behave if in the room

with you now. Start with the physical things, clothes, conversation and how welcome they would be. Go on to imagine their mood, attitude to your house, even what you'd offer them for tea!

- Encourage your child to keep a simple record of what she's reading, particularly sharing the success of good books. Designing a poster or advert for the book could be more fun than writing a review. An artistic child may enjoy drawing a sequence of comic-strip style pictures to show a drama or crisis point in the book. Then use your ignorance of the story to ask her to set the scene in its context, describe the characters, their motives and her sympathy with them.

- Try examining the covers, title and jacket-style of favourite books and redesigning better versions yourselves.

- Use a tape recorder and ask your child to produce a report on the actions of one of the characters, thinking carefully about whose viewpoint she is going to take. This is a difficult task, made easier if you share the drama or humour of what she is trying out.

- Alternatively turn some gripping dialogue into a radio play and then find an appreciative audience who can try and guess the outcome of the drama. Make up a musical soundtrack or a film-release feature showing the strengths of a book which would be great as a TV or big-screen drama. This is a good excuse to go and see some classic dramatised versions yourself.

Developing reference skills

School projects and personal hobbies should give good reasons for using information books. Refer back to page 123 for ideas about the basics involved in looking at reference books together. By this age your child will start to distinguish between information books, reference manuals, dictionaries, encyclopaedias, thesauri, cata-

<u>Furniture Poem</u>   14ᵗʰ October '93

Lindy is the sun emerging from blank
clouds.
She is an overgrown garden, as you
undergrowth cut the undergroth it immediatly
grows back.
She is a grubby block of flats,
underneath, hiding, is a pretty little
cottage.
As a film she would be a neverending
war film.
Her colour is a murky green turning
to the brightness of grass in the summer.
She is a stampeding bull.
She is a flute that will only play
one tune.
"The ink is black, the page is white"
would be her song.
She is a wobbly table.
As a flower she's a daffodil which
droops very easily.
She is a colourless painting of
a woman with moving eyes.
Autumn leaves falling off trees.
She appears to be pale, flat and

PART 5: MOVING OUT: READING INDEPENDENTLY

> inspired, but a dosen looks shows
> her to be a strong fizzy lemonade
> ready to bubble over.
> Lindy is a pencil case with a zip
> that won't close.
>
> Excellent, Louise. You've chosen some
> superb images to describe Lindy.
> You need to come and talk to me
> about the structure of your lines.
> ... and it's Work of the Week for
> the effort you've made with your English
> term well done.
> 18/10/93

Louise used her knowledge of the character to produce these superb images. (There will have been several drafts before this version.)

logues and biographies. The language and style of these books is different to fiction. They are usually read at a different pace or for short bursts depending upon the reason for reading. Unlike fiction, each word may have to be dissected to get accurate and complete information.

What are information retrieval strategies, and how can I help?

This is jargon for getting the answers to the questions your child is asking. Focus on the purpose for reading. This is quite obvious in the case of understanding a word or checking a spelling, but it is harder to have a clear strategy for exploring a general interest. If your child needs to find out a fact or write a section for his project, this gives you a framework for narrowing down your search. Help

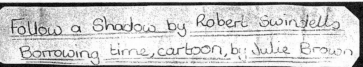

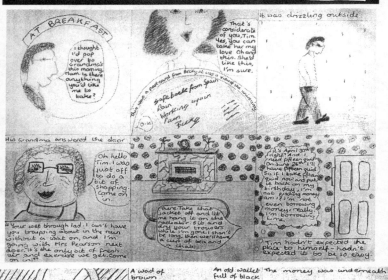

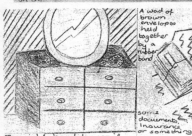

Julie is 12, but her powerful cartoon style can be used by younger readers.

him to approach this differently to when he browses or reads a book from cover to cover. There are two skills he may find particularly useful:

- Skimming is a quick method for getting the gist of the passage. It involves glancing rapidly over a text using the key words to assess whether it is of interest or would be useful to answer specific questions. Your child needs a clear idea of what information he's after and to have the confidence not to get too bogged down with the detail. He should have used the contents page, chapter headings, sub-headings and picture clues to have worked his way to relevant locations. He should also be shown how to use the index to check references to a specific subject.

- Scanning is a fine-tuning process, a way of finding the points needed for careful consideration. Having found the section, your child can use a strategy such as reading the first and concluding sentences of a paragraph to see if he's tracked down what he's after.

Once you've found the hot spots, teach your child ways of using the information rather than copying verbatim. He could copy out key details and compare them with any information he has already. Encourage him to use his own words when re-writing and to ask for help rather than just copying complicated bits! After all this research time it pays to be creative when deciding the best way to present the information. This could be a newspaper report, a logbook, a poem or a cartoon. Talk through the areas your child finds difficult, whether it's finding appropriate facts or writing about them, so that you can offer appropriate help.

How do teachers assess reading ability?

Assessment is a complex but on-going aspect of teaching. The National Curriculum attempts to offer a standardised basis for monitoring progress and to establish guidelines for how that information should be relayed to you.

The teacher's observations

Your child's teacher will obviously spend time hearing your child read, discussing his reading, observing how he applies his skills and assessing his attitude. She will keep careful records diagnosing the type of help needed and summarising his progress. Older children should offer their own observations by identifying areas they would like to improve and talking about their own successes. This can be done in a warm, sharing way with the class, as a group or in private. Encourage your child to share this information with you too. Written reports have a value but parent-teacher meetings are essential to understand what test results and terms actually mean for your child's rate of progress.

Reading lacks the tangible feel of written work, so how do teachers keep records?

The teacher will note how your child settles in to independent reading, the range of books he selects, his favourite authors, his staying power and how long it takes him to finish each book. She will note his response to group reading sessions and whether he shares his opinions about his reading confidently. She looks for evidence of how he uses the knowledge he gains from books. All these strands will be drawn together to compile a reading profile of your child.

Tests and the National Curriculum

Under the National Curriculum children of seven and eleven have a series of set tasks to complete within the school year which will form the basis of Standard Assessment Tasks. These may include such tasks as reading captions around the classroom and using a dictionary independently. Your child will also read a pre-selected passage while the teacher notes what types of mistakes your child makes, how he corrects mistakes, and whether, if he substitutes a word, the word he uses makes sense. Teachers are only allowed to give your child a certain number of words. Finally, the teacher will grade your child's reading for accuracy and will discuss the passage to assess how much he remembers and understands. He may also be asked to focus on the main point of the passage, to retell it in his own words and to predict an outcome. (See chapter 16 for more details about the National Curriculum.)

Examples of different methods of assessment

Cloze passages

These involve your child filling in gaps to make sense of a passage. A short passage, possibly from a familiar text, is given to your child, with every tenth word blanked out. Key words may be listed at the bottom of the page. Children must read carefully, using the context to find meaningful words to make sense of the passage.

Miscue analysis

The teacher listens carefully as your child reads a passage (often pre-set), possibly taping her responses. She then goes through checking all the words your child substituted, marking them according to what approach they show your child was applying. This method requires skilled analysis as your child reads. Pauses, missed words and mistakes (miscued words) are used to assess the strength of your child's different reading strategies.

Sequencing

Children are given a number of sentences or phrases to put in a sensible order. They are then asked to explain why they chose their sequence. Your child has to look for links to form a coherent message.

Modelling

Having read a short passage, your child has to use the main points or features to create a map, diagram chart or other visual response. This can be a useful test of how accurately he reads, understands and applies his knowledge.

Labelling/highlighting

Your child has to invent captions or titles for a passage, so showing that he can skim and focus on the main purpose. Alternatively, he has to highlight key words which provide answers to a series of questions.

Any questions?

Inventing questions is a deceptively difficult task which requires your child to have interpreted and understood the true meaning of the text.

What happens next?

Your child reads a passage and then has to guess at an outcome by using the context intelligently.

Whether reading fact or fiction, you can see how useful it is to help your child focus accurately and to be more specific in how he applies his reading.

Standard tests

What are 'norm-referenced' reading tests?

These tests highlight variations in ability by comparing children to a norm, a yardstick attempting to show a national average. The results are given in reading ages so your child's performance is easily rated. They can provide additional evidence when deciding what support your child needs, but they don't diagnose why your child has registered that reading age.

What are 'criterion-referenced' tests?

Such tests are designed to assess a particular skill or set of skills. This is the philosophy behind many of the Standard Tests in the National Curriculum.

Possible problems with standardised tests

- Concrete figures offer reassurance if good and anxieties when poor.
- They can help diagnose need, but are only a small part of a complex jigsaw.
- Statistics are frequently contradictory and confusing: you need to look at the detail for a clearer picture.
- Different tests claim to measure different skills so we must all be quite clear what they are.
- The tests themselves should interest the age range and experience of the pupils who have to use them, particularly the type of language, vocabulary and context of a passage or list of words.
- A test will only show how your child performed on a particular day in response to just one approach: you don't get clues about your child's rate of progress or how your child actually attempted the task.

Take all these factors into consideration when looking at the cold figures which 'rank' our children.

CHAPTER THIRTEEN

Reading: The final frontier!

Redefining what we mean by reading

The impact of other media

Reading is big news, the subject of speculation about falling standards and declining reading habits. How much of this is scaremongering and how much do we have to accept as a sign of the times? Do we need a wider definition of what we mean by reading which considers a whole range of modern media?

> *In an age of television, videos, computers, sound systems and greater mobility, what is the place of reading for pleasure with our pupils?*
>
> *(A teacher's question, posed as a basis for investigating and nurturing children's reading habits)*

The first priority for parents is to build a daily dose of leisure reading into a busy routine. The squeeze is on as your child juggles an increasing number of outside interests and forms of home entertainment into limited hours. It may be that your child is obsessed with one hobby. A lone child zapping the hours away on his bedroom computer is a depressing sight. But a recent survey suggested that children expect, and might even welcome their parents setting limits for them. We all need different ways to relax, so show your child how reading can be a liberating option. Today's children have a wide range of activity locations (as all parent taxi services know only too well!). Yet bedroom computers and televisions mean children can access the world without opening the door. We need to fight threats to pleasure reading and this can be done partly by using the very things we see as posing that threat.

Accentuate the positive: Using other media to promote reading

Comics and reading

At their best comics offer a fantastic blend of pictures and text. The fast pace, lively action and dialogue can attract children who would otherwise rarely read for pleasure at all. The energy and humour of many classic comics may prompt your child to explore books which adopt a similar style. Good graphic novels show the strength of dialogue and the shape of an adventure story, so try some!

Television and reading: Competition or complementary roles?

Don't blame the demon box for your child's reading lethargy, try to do something about it. If you share at least some viewing time with your child and help him become selective about what he watches, you will both get satisfaction from television.

There are some excellent educational programmes, easily missed as they are on during the day, which offer language delights and learning points. At the youngest end of the scale, some programmes feature good picture books. They draw out themes and emphasise phonics and word recognition. Children love seeing books come

Horton Tower.

Hi my name is Tim. I want to tell you about when I went to Hoton Tower I sneaked out of my room, got my bike and rode up to Horton Tower. When I got there I saw a full moon. I shut the door of Horton Tower. Suddenly somebody hit me. A dark shadow moved forward. It stopped, I heard the sound of jet engines it was THUNDEBIRD 1. Scott Tracy had come to save me! BANG! the shadow fell, Scott whisked me off to Tracy. Island and balk bome. That night I went to investigate. I opened the door and fell down a trap door. !AAAAHHHH! There bones everywhere. It was horrible. I trampled over the bones. Ther was a tunnel ahead.

I squeezed through, At the end of the tunnel there was a mad genius working on a killer robot. I did not like the look of this, The robot moved, I was frantic. I ran in, grabbed an axe and smashed the machine up. The man was very angry. It was easier said than done lopping his head off. I smashed up all the equipment so nobody else could take over, I squeezed back thoought the tunnel, over the bones, climbed up the trap door opening and straight out of the door, then I woke up.

By Timothy Crook.

Timothy's love of Thunderbirds helped to blast off his imagination!

to life, while you can pick up ideas for new authors and titles to try.

Junior English programmes deal with a whole range of styles, skills and approaches covering both reading and writing. The school may be able to recommend specific programmes together with relevant books and resources.

After-school television has frequent examples of programmes rooted in books, they just take tracking down.

Books linked to television and films

When children are free to choose and buy books for themselves, for example at a school book fair, they are drawn to covers which are linked to television. This ranges from Gladiators, Sonic, Postman Pat, Thunderbirds and The Animals of Farthing Wood, to a dramatic surge in the popularity of Mary Wesley's *The Borrowers* after a brilliant BBC adaptation. Some of these choices are popular with us parents, so perhaps we should accept the less savoury options too. At least your child is happily keeping up a reading habit which could give her the confidence and motivation to move to other books. Disney books, for example, come in a range of formats, so find one which matches her reading level and see her curled up enjoying a real book! (see the Appendix on page 235).

Helping less able readers

Television gives children a chance to enjoy longer, more complex novels before they can read them independently. Younger children learn about story structure and discover worlds of new ideas. Familiar characters, flights of imagination, and interesting facts are easily digested in a way which could draw your child back to books.

Computer games

OK, it's the zapping games which top the sales figures, but there are programmes which can actually promote reading and writing (refer to the Appendix on page 215 for sources of recent information). Like television viewing, if you guide your child, limit the sessions and offer entertaining packages, the computer can work for both of you. On the reading side there are games which help familiarity with letter sounds, label objects and which present animated texts of reading books. Your child can then practise again and again at her own pace in an entertaining and non-threatening way. Most complex, problem-solving games involve a degree of reading, but there are programmes which deal specifically with interpreting longer fiction, developing study skills and reading for meaning. There are also excellent supports for children with special needs.

The word-processing package is a life-saver for those who find handwriting and spelling particularly stressful. There are attractive ways of editing and laying out text which can motivate your child to write. Many programmes aim to give a structure for creative writing, or to promote a certain style of writing. One of the most popular is one which allows your child to play the role of Reporter. Whatever your child's particular interests, there's likely to be a relevant game which involves him in reading and writing. Your child can also help you overcome fears and phobias, so that you too become a computer-literate member of society!

Whatever media we use and however widely we might define reading, we want our children to be drawn to books because of the sense of pleasure and purpose they find there. If this means altering our preconceptions about 'proper books' it may be a small price to pay for creating a life-long reading habit. We must use the weapons of today to fight for our children's attention.

What about those worrying surveys and statistics?

A recent survey implied that of all the three Rs, reading at school had declined in popularity the most, compared with the children's grandparents' generation. A 22 per cent decline in the popularity of reading at school was matched by an 11 per cent reduction in reading for pleasure. The only region to consistently resist this trend was Scotland.

Gloomy survey results always make good news, perhaps without too much thought being given to the size of the sample, or how the data was collected. Children of this age-range will readily trot out 'Books are boring', as the 'in' thing to say. Relate what you read to what you see your child doing and talk to his teacher about ways of stopping the rot. This survey also drew attention to the time pressure on leisure activities which we've already discussed.

Conflicting reports about declining reading standards tend to breed defensiveness and confusion. Are we expecting more of readers today, with frequent swings and changes in any job structure and with increasingly refined communication skills required in all types of work? The statistical evidence available from testing at seven implies that a quarter of the children are failing to reach targets in reading, and that even more fail to reach writing standards. But how do we get these results? One of the difficulties is that a factor such as complications in converting to joined writing by seven can create a distorted picture overall. National Curriculum bands are broad and potentially misleading. We must look very carefully and avoid a panic reaction. We should also relate this picture to what goes on in the adult reading world.

What do surveys tell us about adult attitudes to reading and writing?

The National Literacy Trust was founded in September 1993, with far-reaching aims to promote good practice in the teaching and learning of literacy. One of its priorities, as stressed by Neil McClelland, the Trust's full-time director, is to show the importance of parental involvement in developing literacy. In their survey, 97 per cent of the parents questioned saw that their individual help and encouragement was critical to their child's development. Nearly as many were prepared to volunteer some free time to help their children learn to read and write, but some lacked sufficient encouragement and direction from schools.

What did the Trust's survey reveal about attitudes to reading and writing? Although adults agreed upon the enduring importance of reading, they saw it in mainly functional terms, with only 45 per cent of men describing reading as relaxing. Though 89 per cent of the adults questioned read newspapers at least once a week, only 35 per cent read fiction for pleasure at least once a week. We must examine our own reading habits and the messages they give to our children, particularly if we expect them to enjoy reading as a hobby. Even more alarming was that 30 per cent of men in a sample of over a thousand adults never read fiction. (Boys' attitudes to reading and writing require more careful handling, hunting down inviting books and finding interesting reasons for writing. Girls are far more inclined to do this voluntarily and independently, and to read more widely.)

Adult responses to questions about writing were also illuminating. They identified skills such as spelling, handwriting and 'stringing sentences together to get a point or series of ideas across'. But very few had jobs which required any complex use of writing and most felt reading to be a more important skill. Sadly, although the need to write a few words was seen as essential for everyday survival, hardly any adults took pleasure in writing. This makes it harder to encourage our children to write spontaneously and to seek enjoyment from expressing their own ideas.

Let the children have the last word

Whatever negative evidence you may find, take heart from some children who do get pleasure from reading:

> ❝ I enjoy reading for pleasure because it's a time when you can just relax and block out the rest of the world. ❞
>
> *(Ben)*

> ❝ I enjoy reading because I can just shut myself away in a fantasy land and imagine pictures. I'd imagine I was there but invisible. ❞
>
> *(Elizabeth)*

> ❝ I like reading for pleasure because it helps me relax. If I've had a tiring day, a book helps to calm me down. Some books I enjoy reading over and over, some only once or twice. I prefer to read in bed but not on a schoolday morning because it's usually so hectic. ❞
>
> *(Christopher, with all the cares of the world on his shoulders at 11!)*

> ❝ I enjoy reading before I go to bed at night because it takes my mind off everything else and my imagination is fresh. ❞
>
> *(Michael)*

> ❝ The books I like to read give me pleasure and sometimes give me a change of mind. ❞
>
> *(Carla)*

Adults too can have a passionate need for reading:

> ❝ Reading helps me to enjoy each day of my life without hitting a brick wall and stopping to think what to do next. ❞
>
> *(Woman in her 40s responding to a survey by the National Literacy Trust)*

CHAPTER FOURTEEN

Writing them off in the final years?

Like reading, writing is a staple part of almost every element in the curriculum. You will want to see evidence that your child's skills measure up to the challenge of producing flowing prose in a variety of styles. His writing should be readable and an accurate reflection of what he wants to say.

> ❝ *I've finished. That's all I want to say.* ❞

You may detect a discrepancy between his reading level, his oral skills and his willingness to write in depth. By this stage there can be some pretty sophisticated avoidance strategies to counter! It isn't just laziness which steers some children to offer the minimum they think they can get away with. There are complex attitudes, misconceptions, even phobias about writing. Many children who find writing a trial, seek their own solutions:

> ❝ *He is beginning to object to having to write things,*
> *and is looking for the shortest way of saying*
> *something.* ❞
>
> (parent of a son, aged ten)

Only by working with his school and finding enjoyable reasons for writing, can you hope to shift his opinion without negative pressure.

Ideas outlined in earlier chapters should help older reluctant writers too.

Having the confidence to take control and face the challenges

Writing needs staying power and enthusiasm to succeed. For children who are over the initial challenges of joined up writing and who have a large sight vocabulary, surely life should get easier? In fact the range of different ways your child has to apply his skills, and the complexity and length of what he's aiming for, ensure that he will still feel stretched. By this stage drafting and editing will be a logical part of much of his work, particularly when intended for a book or special display. This process requires time, something a busy primary curriculum can't always offer in sufficient quantities.

Your child needs to see himself as being someone who has sway over what and how he writes and who takes responsibility for evaluating his own work. Freedom of expression isn't easy to achieve in a classroom where a certain amount of standard work must be covered and time is carefully rationed. Free, enthusiastic writing opportunities at home give a balance to the school diet. A careful analysis of school work with your child should highlight areas where he wants more support. You can't suddenly compensate by this stage, but patience and a readiness to share the joys of writing through tapping his interests should help.

In the classroom

By now your child will take a more active role in assessing his own writing progress. A 'writing conference' is a rather grand term used to describe sessions talking over recent work. The teacher will then be able to assess where your child needs help, his attitude towards

HELP YOUR CHILD WITH READING AND WRITING

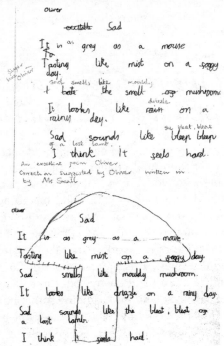

Oliver

~~exitable~~ Sad

It is as grey as a mouse
Tasting like mist on a soggy day.
It ~~hate~~ the smell of mushroom.
It looks like drizzle rain on a rainy day.
Sad sounds like bleep bleep
I think It seels hard.

An excellent poem Oliver.
Corrections suggested by Oliver written in by Ms Small

Oliver

Sad

It is as grey as a mouse.
Tasting like mist on a ~~soggy~~ day.
Sad smells like mouldy mushroom.
It looks like drizzle on a rainy day.
Sad sounds like the bleat, bleat of a lost lamb.
I think It seels hard.

The Fire Bird

Hungry heat claws reach out for prey,

As the wind howls the inferno strikes the helpless victim,

Lava filled wings streak with venomous glee, towards the helpless prisoner of fire,

While a toxic cloak of darkness envelopes all life,

Screeches of curse every atom,
A flash combs the ground,
For death destruction to be found.

by
Luke Trotman

Luke Trotman

Draft 1 + 2

Hungry heat claws reaching out for vegetation prey,
As the wind blows howls the inferno strikes the helpless victim.
Lava filled wings streak with venomous glee.
Toxic dust envelopes all life in a cloak of darkness.
The heart of the flames, a piercing knife
With screeches of death which gins no life

Reaching
Prey
inferno
strikes
helpless
victim
lava
wings
streak
venom
Toxic
envelopes
heart
flames
piercing
knife
screach
death

These are fantastic poems achieved after hours of rewriting and debate.

PART 5: WRITING THEM OFF IN THE FINAL YEARS?

different tasks, his confidence and motivation. They can then agree a way ahead to develop specific skills.

Through his reading your child should have the chance to discuss quality writing: classic opening paragraphs, ways of building up atmosphere, detailed descriptions and lively dialogue. This should help him relate these qualities back to his own writing.

Night move

The gate swings on it hinges
The boarded up windows
are like blank staring eyes
No colour, no light
lifeless

His eyes widen in fright,
hands sweating,
heart thumps,
he edged onwards.

Dampsteps shine with moisture,
paint peels from posts and ledges
Dead leaves rustle,
blown round by the wind

A chilling breeze creeps round him,
like whispers down his neck
Sends a shiver down his spine
He falls, catching his bag,

He limps towards the door
then stops
Not daring to go on
Not wanting to turn back

The door opens slowly
He drifts through
unable to stop himself
unable to turn back

He sees the beast,
staring at him
A black tail flickers at his lips
The beast grabs it and starts pulling
The black, scaly body shines,
in the dim light.

Silence
He stops not able to move,
his feet glued to the floor
Everything swirls round him

This poem is loaded with dramatic tension and atmosphere.

When you go to look at his work, ask open-ended questions to find out the thinking behind the words. Focus on areas he has been particularly successful in and emphasise his progress. At the same time, note areas of weakness which you might be able to help with later.

At home

Talking time ... continued!

Many of the skills associated with writing can be practised orally. For example, rather like reading study skills, your child needs a systematic approach to writing and organising his ideas. He must use his language skills to structure his thoughts within a workable framework. You don't want to threaten the individual way your child responds, particularly to creative tasks. But it's useful to help him know how to get going, especially when you consider the time pressure at school. If your child likes to ease into work slowly or he can't bear the thought of writing anything wrong, he has these barriers to overcome before he can free his ideas.

Give specific tips about getting started, great opening ideas and approaches such as brainstorming. This is where your child has to record as many words or ideas as possible on a subject in a few minutes. Oral quickfire games with no threat of failure and the challenge of improving their own skills work well with many children. One of the most common approaches is to think of as many words as possible on a particular theme for one minute, then to share them with others.

Reasons for writing ... by your children

When I asked children to describe their favourite writing activities, the answer was almost always 'stories' because:

❝ *I can write what I like, I like getting the excitement.* ❞

❝ *They can be happy or sad.* ❞

❝ *... sometimes my imaginative mind runs away with me.* ❞

(Kathryn, 9)

PART 5: WRITING THEM OFF IN THE FINAL YEARS?

Autumn.

1. The sky was a whirlpool.
2. The spiders webs was glistening and beauliful. *beautiful*
3. The frost glistened merrily on the bracken.
4. The leaves were crunchy and it was like you were in a cloud.
5. The dew was sparkling briittle and cold.
6. The shaclows were long and thin. *shadows*
7. The sun was not very strong. *use one word*
8. The tree on the hill was the gorgans.
9. All different trees were hair brushes. *different*
10. The birds were all higgledy *higgledy piggledy*
11. Humans were all cold, frosen to the bone. *frozen*

Laura's draft is deft and keenly observed.

> ❝ *I like writing stories because I like to set my mind adrift.* ❞
>
> (Alex, 10)

> ❝ *I like writing fiction stories because I can write superhuman things about the characters.* ❞
>
> (Peter, 10)

These comments bring home the thrill and excitement of using your imagination. The content of some of the examples of children's work shows the quality of their language skills.

Help your child enjoy a wide range of story types. You could look for favourite examples of the following: fairy tale and folk tale, myths and legends, fables, fantasy, mystery and adventure stories. Themes such as school and animal stories and those with a historical setting are worth investigating. Science fiction, thrillers, horror and crime writing are particularly popular. Introduce her to biographies and autobiographies of heroines linked to her hobbies. Learning to distinguish different styles in reading should lend variety and confidence to her writing.

Support areas where she has particular problems. This could be opening sentences, detailed description, or the difference between her personal response and imagining something from a character's point of view. By talking through how characters behave in her stories you can help create a more rounded, detailed picture.

Helping with presentation skills is still important. Refer to chapter 6, and pages 147 and 200.

Pleas for the pleasures of poetry

For some reason many of us fight shy of poetry. Perhaps we feel unable to offer much to our children because we're no good at it ourselves. This is a shame, because poetry has enormous qualities to offer. It is not the rarefied stuff we may remember, but an exciting and controlled way of dealing with everyday events and emotions. Poetic writing can have a strong influence on a child's prose style.

If your child expresses an interest in poetry, try to get involved yourself. There is such a fascinating array of collections, from the rude, the side-splitting and the clever, to the emotional, sensitive and beautifully apt. Just a few words can create a rich vision or a raw emotion. Children recognise that poetry brings out the need to limit and control words, to work through a clear sense of purpose to produce a pattern and completeness.

> ❝ *I like writing poetry because you have got to write it in a different way to normal.* ❞
>
> (Gemma)

PART 5: WRITING THEM OFF IN THE FINAL YEARS?

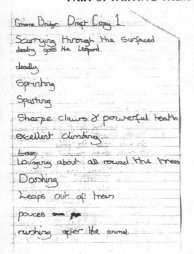

Graeme Bridger Draft Copy 1

Scurrying through the surfaced
deadly goes the Leopard.

deadly

Sprinting

Spurting

Sharpe claws & powerful teath

excellent climbing

Lazy
Lounging about all round the trees

Dashing

Leaps out of trees

pouces on go

rushing after the animal.

Sprinting through the trees,
The fire bites through
anything.
Still spurting through the
undergroth goes the speeding
fire unstopaable as it may
seem.
Climbing up the trees as fast
as can be.
Still keeps on going no sign
of tire.
Still with the whirling wind
blowing the fire further and
further on.
No time to stop just keep
jumping from tree to tree
sending them up in flames.

By Graeme Bridger.

Look where a 'simple' list can lead.

None of these skills grow overnight and some children respond more easily than others. If the motivation is there, get reading aloud, talking and creating! Start by making an anthology of poems you particularly enjoy. These will produce a whole range of models and ideas to discuss. List-like responses, maybe to a colour or an emotion, are a lovely way to get started.

Have fun with riddles and teasers and draw out your child's love of alliteration. A younger child might offer a 'terrible tiger' whilst an older child has more complex ideas such as the tiger's 'taunting talons'. Firm up alliterative skills by producing a whole alphabet from 'alluring apples' to 'zany zebras'. An alphabet of sounds and noisy words provides further ideas for the sort of lively language used by poets! You can also encourage your child to build up descriptive skills and to observe detail, perhaps by having a mysterious object to handle. Older children can use such powers to describe moods and feelings.

Poetry also helps with appreciating rhyme, rhythm and syllables. Japanese Haiku poems are a good example as they are based on

HELP YOUR CHILD WITH READING AND WRITING

only seventeen syllables. Composing them requires careful control and reworking. You wouldn't believe the amount of effort required for three or four deceptively simple lines! (If your child is unfamiliar with syllables, do plenty of counting and clapping first.)

These Haiku poems by 9–10-year-olds vividly reveal the impact concealed in a mere three lines:

Loneliness
Is the silence
of the world being broken
by strange thoughts of sadness?
(Clare)

Death
The feeling of death
was like soaring through swirling
time warps of darkness.
(Alison)

Sunset
Blazing and shining
the red sun set on concrete
like splashes of paint.
(Georgina)

Pain
A boulder crushing you
and squashing you like putty
Crunching your bones.
(Michael)

The shape, size and, most importantly, the sounds of words, make poetry a perfect source from which to tap phonetic skills, too. At the same time your child can learn about the different types of words in a phrase: action words, with adverbs to provide detail, and nouns with adjectives to describe them. With all this to offer and the chance for tongue-twisting wordplay, I'm sure your child could get hooked on poems of some sort.

❨ *I like writing poetry because my poems never make sense.* ❩

(Katherine, 10)

Functional writing

Writing has to work for a living too. From holiday cards to shopping lists, thank you letters to memos, everyday family life is littered with examples of more functional writing. Encourage your child to explore these possibilities using a tape or typewriter to vary production. Start by helping him sort out what style of writing fits his purpose. For example, a letter to a firm requesting a free information pack must be differently phrased to his per.-pal letter. Letters show the need for paragraphs and a clear order in our message. From an introduction, to the meat of the message, and a few closing gestures, your child will enjoy being professional, and receiving an appropriate reply! Use your local paper, cereal packet offers, competitions and special interest clubs as other sources of business letter writing.

Surveys at school can get your child doing similar market research at home. This could be a simple 'What's your favourite programme/meal/drink?' questionnaire, or one tackling more complex issues. Perhaps your child feels strongly about bedtime rules or where she's allowed to play. A carefully compiled survey between friends and neighbours, honestly recorded, could produce interesting results for all of you! Of course, you must be prepared to take issues further if you want your sleuth to feel her efforts are worthwhile!

Look at newspaper reports on subjects which are likely to captivate your child. Draw her attention to the style, the length of the feature and how the information is used. Look at the opening sentence and the headline to decide how it attracts the reader. Your child may later want to produce reports on family or local matters. If you have access to a word processor, you can give her the satisfaction of seeing a carefully reworked piece printed in a realistic layout.

HELP YOUR CHILD WITH READING AND WRITING

Inside Buddys head.

There is a safe full of Ideas ready
to burst open,
And a kettle boiling up all his anger.
There is a framed picture showing
the best moment of his life
And an ugly painting showing the
worst
There is a wish that his mum would
come home,
And a hope that his Dad would
start his shop up again.
There is a rainbow full of
feelings
And a bin containing all his bad
thoughts.
Theres a grave with Buddys
name scratched upon it
And a time bomb ticking away
his life.

Two accomplished poets with contrasting styles.

PART 5: WRITING THEM OFF IN THE FINAL YEARS?

<u>Homeguard</u>

The Homeguard captured German airman when their planes were forced down.
They were a force of volounteers who served in their spare time.

<u>Anderson shelter</u>

A hole dug in the gound. They were covered in corrugatted iron.

<u>Wartime Rationing—Ration Books.</u>

Ration books contained pages and pages of coupons. Shop clipped off coupons against whatever they supplied.

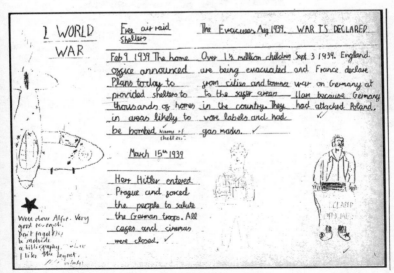

1 WORLD WAR	<u>Free air raid shelters</u>	The Evacuees Aug 1939. WAR IS DECLARED
	Feb 9 1939 The home office announced plans today to provided shelters to thousands of homes in areas likely to be bombed. <small>Name of shelters</small>	Over 1½ million children are being evacuated from cities and towns to the safer areas in the country. They wore labels and had gas masks. ✓
	March 15th 1939	Sept 3 1939. England and France declare war on Germany. at 11am because Germany had attacked Poland. ✓
	Herr Hitler entered Prague and forced the people to salute the German troops. All cages and cinemas were closed. ✓	

Well done Alfie. Very good research. Don't forget to include a bibliography. I like the layout.

Alfie and Stephen set out their research beautifully.

HELP YOUR CHILD WITH READING AND WRITING

Newspapers can also get you going on interviews and on using a tape to record opinions or get eye-witness accounts. It's then up to your editor and the other hacks to produce an accurate feature.

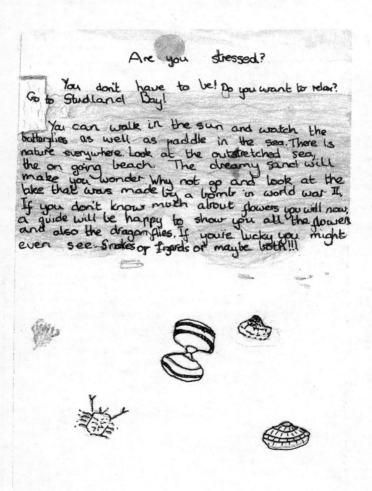

> Are you stressed?
>
> You don't have to be! Do you want to relax? Go to Studland Bay!
>
> You can walk in the sun and watch the butterflies as well as paddle in the sea. There is nature everywhere. Look at the outstretched sea, the on going beach. The dreamy sand will make you wonder Why not go and look at the like that was made by a bomb in world war II, If you don't know much about flowers you will now, a guide will be happy to show you all the flowers and also the dragonflies. If you're lucky you might even see snakes or lizards or maybe both!!!

A ten-year-old attempts persuasive writing – and convinces me I need a break!

This is excellent for thinking about punctuation, reported speech and the difference between fact and opinion. Use humour and persuasive writing to earn some revenue for your paper with lively adverts.

If you have a tape recorder, adapt some of these ideas and go in for radio production too.

Where do the rules fit in?

As long as your child is writing freely, spontaneously and enthusiastically in a variety of forms, the opportunities for applying spelling, punctuation and grammar rules will evolve naturally. You will need to sort out with her the main areas of weakness and then allow regular and entertaining ways to practise skills. Most children are acutely aware of their problems with spelling, grammar and punctuation.

> ❝ I would like to improve my handwriting and style because my style isn't that amazing. ❞
>
> (Laura, 9)

> ❝ I think my detail needs to be better. I am not very good but I am getting better gradually. ❞
>
> (Peggitty-Ann, 9)

> ❝ I would like to improve my spelling because it is poor. ❞
>
> (Peter, 11)

> ❝ I want to be neater, take more time over my work and use the dictionary more. ❞
>
> (Timothy, 9)

Work together to provide practical support by whatever means work for your child.

Knowing what 'good writing' is

Changes in the National Curriculum have resulted in increased emphasis upon Standard English. It is important that your child learns what rules of style, presentation and grammar are required in more formal writing. However, this should not suppress her individualism, nor limit her creative energies. Extensive reading will help your child appreciate that conversational tones do not fit all forms of writing and so adapt her style accordingly.

Presentation practice for older writers

In addition to the editing and spelling support already mentioned, try some of these ideas:

- When checking spellings try reading from the end of the piece as this will force attention on individual words. This highlights careless mistakes which are easily missed when you know what it ought to say! Use the backwards approach to correct silly errors and underline other words you're not sure of. Remind your child of ways to check spellings, and go through the 'look, cover, write, check' routine (see page 74) with those that you agree need particular attention.

- Keep a quickfire quiz book of tricky spellings to memorise and check them regularly.

- Remind your child of other ways to improve spelling, such as building up larger words from a base, or knocking down a larger word to find its component parts. Seeing patterns is an important part of spelling. Puzzles, crosswords, grids and wordplay games will be helping spelling awareness.

- Dictionary work, and knowing the meaning and origin of words, also aid spelling sophistication. There are excellent junior thesauri available to widen vocabulary and stimulate a healthy interest in words.

- Remembering spelling rules is likely to be a problem for the children who need them most. These rules have a value when visual patterns are unclear, or when the correct spelling is linked to recognising sounds, such as distinguishing 'hopping' and 'hoping'! Word-ending rules are useful but require an understanding of syllables and vowels.

- Knowing a rule, and applying it correctly, do not unfortunately follow on naturally. Make rules work for you by linking them in as the need arises when you are editing work together.

- Mnemonics or memory sentences are a fun way of remembering otherwise indigestible facts. Your child will also get some entertainment out of inventing his own zany collection of memory-joggers.

- Make a list of Sophisticated Spelling Slip-Ups: all those words which trip everyone up. Set your child a target of learning one such word a week and then testing him a week later.

- Design attractive but practical posters or sheets listing tricky words related to projects or subject areas, like 'equals' for Maths and 'microscope' for Science.

- Games, such as making as many words as possible from 'parliament' or 'information', focus attention on letter patterns and the structure of words. Try more sophisticated and useful versions of Hangman, such as insisting the letters are guessed in their correct order.

Whatever methods you use to aid spelling, do remember to write things down so she can see that it looks right. Keeping things lively and relevant removes the drudgery and tyranny that spellings hold for many of us.

The art of book-making

One way to stimulate quality writing is to produce some books of your own. Because 'real' books are so professional we tend to be put off attempting home-spun varieties. In fact you need very little technical knowledge, just your child's creative energy and some basic materials. There are several books around which provide examples of the range and styles you could explore, from origami to folded concertina books.

Self-made books stimulate good writing because they are personal, special and require effort. Encourage any interest your child shows by exploring different forms and experimenting to find the most suitable paper and materials. Books provide a reason for careful planning and control; they help writers by setting physical limits on how much they need to write. A well-matched style instantly lifts the text and adds to the value of your child's writing. Most books will be prompted by a particular occasion or made for special audience, giving further status to the writing. Book-making opens out the process of writing to include other visual and creative skills. This gives confidence to children who will not readily write but who love to doodle with cartoon characters. Don't worry if your own artistic skills never got off the drawing board – your child's enthusiasm is what counts!

Good writing is never easy. After a demanding day at school it's understandable that most children prefer bikes and balls to pens. If your child wants to work, she deserves your support and encouragement whether the shortfalls of what she produces. Only when a writing habit is secure should you scrutinise the quality more closely. Above all, your child should enjoy writing and be able to express her thoughts confidently. These foundations will give her a secure base for her later schooling.

CHAPTER FIFTEEN

Moving out: Easing the strain of transferring to secondary school

Most children face a major change of schooling at the age of eleven. There are regional variations, such as middle schools which take pupils from eight or nine until the age of thirteen. Whatever the age of transfer, change is on the way. For a start, your child could be going from a small primary school of under a hundred pupils where she is amongst the eldest and elite, to a school of perhaps over a thousand pupils of whom she's amongst the most vulnerable. Many schools establish strong links, to ease transfer and to encourage continuity. Despite these initiatives some disruption is inevitable, so your child is likely to need far more support for a while.

What changes will my child have to cope with?

Size of school

This affects the day-to-day logistics of getting around from lesson to lesson, knowing where to go for help and information and coping with the sheer size and volume of older pupils. Many children with language-learning difficulties will find this more daunting because of the strain on memory, orientation and interpreting written instructions.

Changes in friendship patterns and the social side of school

This of course varies greatly: it may be that your child's close friends are still together. Even so, groups are likely to be organised differently, the journey to school may well be longer and 'playtimes' will feel strange. More freedom will be linked with greater responsibility.

Hours of work

The school day may well be longer, particularly with the likelihood of increased journey time. Time at home is reduced, and you both have less mental energy after you've battled to complete official homework!

Range of studies

Many primary schools cover subject areas partly within projects. The range of subjects is similar at secondary school (although your child may be learning a second language for the first time), but the presentation is different. It feels strange simply because it is more segmented.

Subject teachers and form teachers

Most children will have been used to having one teacher for the majority of teaching time. There was no confusion as to whom to turn to for help. Now your child will have subject specialists and a separate teacher, even group of teachers, for pastoral care. She must learn whom to approach for different needs.

Having homework

Many primary schools set spelling tests and encourage older pupils to take work home. Much of this was probably research for projects, finishing things off, or informal requests. Secondary teaching puts homework on a formal footing with a diary of regular evenings for different subjects. Help your child get organised and to feel positive about what she may sense is an intrusion into her free time. Homework must somehow be slotted into your after-school life so that it doesn't compete with her favourite television programme or her hobbies. Whether your child agrees with the comfort of getting it out of the way, or needs persuasion to limit her hobby-time, completing everything with a smile is an impossible dream.

Emphasise the positive by sharing in and extending things that interest her, and guide her as painlessly as possible over trouble spots. If this fails, your constant glares should help focus on GETTING IT DONE!

Marking

Work may be marked differently. Written grades, corrections and comments are essential when the staff only see their pupils for a few sessions a week. This is fine when your child has a string of 'Excellent, Well Done' 'A' grades, but much harder for both of you when hit with the 'D's. Any negative comments should be tempered and have something constructive to build on. Boost your child's confidence when you know he's tried hard and emphasise positive comments. You both have to be realistic about his ability: few of us are lucky enough to be good at everything. But you need reassurance that he cares about his own progress, that he's not losing confidence or feeling miserable about himself. Children can be very competitive, but help convert this into positive energy rather than low motivation.

Is English taught differently?

Find out how frequently English features on her timetable and the breakdown into different areas of study, such as library work, studying literature and formal written work. Some of the sessions may be double periods requiring sustained concentration. Those afternoons spent helping your child get organised to develop her writing independently, or listening to stories will be well rewarded! The reassuring news is that many of the processes and objectives will be the same. There will be increasing refinement, but your rounded home support is still useful. Staff will expect your child to be self-disciplined about keeping up records, setting herself targets and developing a regular reading habit. They will want her to take a pride in facing new challenges in her written work.

The energy and enthusiasm to enjoy reading and writing comes from a multitude of sources. So keep the house littered with entertaining opened books, zany games and materials for writing. Get out and talk about the rich experiences which colour a young world. Show your child that you care about her progress and pleasure in reading and writing and that you are always willing to help. As the problems become tougher, so you will both truly be part of a shared learning experience!

Home–school links

The size of secondary schools makes it harder but more crucial to keep up effective links. Many primary and secondary schools are moving towards class or year-based organisations for parents. They can then offer you regular curriculum reviews, termly forecasts and even weekly surgeries to address your specific concerns. Such measures take time and understanding to reap results, but it is our children who should benefit.

CHAPTER SIXTEEN

The National Curriculum

For an intimate link with the National Curriculum and concrete evidence of how it affects your child, go and see your child's teacher! Every school has manuals for you to browse through or borrow and staff available to clarify points. You don't need to wade through the dry details though; how your child is getting on is what matters. But it does help to appreciate the framework the National Curriculum gives, and its objectives, also how and when testing occurs and possible ways you can help at home.

Back to basics: What is the National Curriculum and to whom does it apply?

The National Curriculum became law in 1988. It covers all pupils in state schools in England and Wales (Scotland has a separate educational system). Special schools are included, as are schools which have opted out, but independent schools and CTCs (city technology colleges) are not covered. The ideals behind a national curriculum stem from a concern to improve educational standards for all pupils and to ensure that everyone involved in your child's education speaks the same language. By clearly stating what subjects need to be taught and for what goals we are aiming, it should make it easier to assess and improve standards. Putting these ideals into practice is far from simple, although most people have welcomed the efforts to achieve a more balanced and broad curriculum.

What is a curriculum?

A curriculum covers the whole school experience not just the facts and figures. The way your child learns is as important. Mature study skills, together with an ability to apply her learning, help relate her education to future demands as a working adult. A curriculum has to be broad enough to promote your child's moral, spiritual, mental, cultural and physical development. A tall order! Equally demanding is that a curriculum must also be specific enough to cover the key areas of learning. So it is hardly surprising that there has been a need to modify and update the curriculum to achieve something workable and useful.

How is the present National Curriculum organised?

The first thing to note is that we are still in the early days of the National Curriculum, and it is still being worked on. It is important, therefore, that you make sure you get up to date information – the best source is probably your child's teacher.

Earlier this year (1994) the findings of the Dearing Report were largely accepted by Government and teachers, resulting in a substantial slimming down of an overloaded curriculum. In the early years of education the aim is to focus firmly on basic skills, which are now more clearly defined. The time freed by the slimming-down process should be used to reach this objective. The English Orders set out teaching methods by which targets outlined in the curriculum can be achieved. You need to understand the terms to appreciate how things are organised:

The curriculum is divided into three core subjects, of which

English is one (the others being Maths and Science). There are additional foundation subjects – which are still compulsory, but which are allocated less teaching time – such as History and Geography. Whilst much primary teaching may still be done through themes and topics, far greater attention has to be paid to the amount of teaching time allocated to each subject. This can create limitations, but there is a clear effort to ensure balance and that a standard emphasis is shared by all schools.

Aims, goals and assessment

The National Curriculum links assessment, both through observation and standard tests, to achievement of targets. Thus English is subdivided into Attainment Targets (ATs), which are graded into different levels. There are now three targets for English:

AT1 Speaking and Listening covering communication, listening and responding;

AT2 Reading covering initial reading skills (for Levels 1 to 3), comprehension, response to literature and information handling;

AT3 Writing covering composition, writing in different styles for different purposes, grammar, punctuation, spelling and handwriting.

Each area is further divided into Levels of Attainment, which set out the learning to be achieved through Statements of Attainment. Children develop through these Levels at their own pace. However, there are Key Stages at which point Standard Tests have to be completed by all pupils. Testing and assessment goes on all the time: these Key Stages are just benchmark years for national assessment. The jargon easily confuses, but basically most children follow the same pattern:

Reception Year when your child is five, is spent working towards Level 1;

Years 1 and 2 at school cover the ages of six and seven, during which the children work towards **Key Stage 1**. By the end of these years, most children will be working at Level 2, with some on Level 1 and some on Level 3.

Key Stage 2, the next major benchmark, covers the Years 3 to 6 at school, so pupils are tested again in the year they are 11. By then it is thought that most pupils will be working between Levels 3 and 5, although individual progress may fall anywhere within a seven-year ability range. The idea is not to limit but to provide an effective means of monitoring progress.

Don't be drawn by talk about 'straightforward and rigorous tests' into becoming anxious or wanting to prepare your child. The pressures during these Key years are on teachers' time rather than children. Belatedly, the number of Key Stage 1 tests has been reduced and simplified so that far greater emphasis is placed on the teacher's assessment profile. At Key Stage 1 your child is likely to have to answer questions on a passage, as described on page 175. After Level 2, there may be more emphasis on written comprehension, but the exact format is subject to revision. So far only pilot studies have been conducted for tests at Key Stage 2, but by 1995 there should be a clearer picture of what's involved.

Monitoring progress always has been a crucial part of education. In the same way, concerns about standards and 'Standard English' are a constant facet of debate about language learning. It is for educationalists to find the most effective means to judge and measure progress.

Can the National Curriculum help me to help my child?

The statements are there to define what pupils should understand, know or do at each Level. Examples are given to clarify each objective but these can be rather confusing. For instance, the Reading

Target includes a statement at Level 3 which asserts that your child should be able to 'Read aloud from familiar stories and poems fluently and with appropriate expression'. Terms such as 'familiar', 'fluently' and 'appropriate' are subjective and open to different interpretation. So the examples, whilst providing some guidance, can also be rather misleading, particularly to those of us who don't have to interpret them on a daily basis!

The curriculum document will show you what areas are given greatest emphasis and will give details of what is meant by terms such as 'Standard English'. There are even lists of useful reading material, although the books quoted are given as examples and are not compulsory. This shouldn't inhibit the type of reading you enjoy with your child. The best source of support should be your child's teacher, so do all you can to retain positive links with the school.

The whole message of this book has been to draw out the unique value and pleasures of home learning. Beware! It is tempting to use the changes in the Curriculum as a means of supporting the central role of phonics or of arguing the importance that is given to 'Standard English'. This should never be done by sacrificing the core value of balance, or by ignoring the plea to ensure learning is relevant and meaningful.

The National Curriculum focuses firmly upon introducing our children to a broad range of interesting content and on promoting positive attitudes to learning. All these messages support the efforts you make at home with your child. Don't get lost behind the Statements and Attainment Targets; your role remains central to your child's success. Childish as it may seem, you are best promoting and sharing in the pleasures of your child's progress.

My message is to make learning fun.
I KNOW that it's easier said than done (especially with some)!
But don't let anything others say
Take your caring knowledge of your child away.

Useful organisations

Sources of information about children's books

Organisations

Books for Keeps 6 Brightfield Road, Lee, London, SE12 8QF. Tel: 081 852 4953. Produces an informative bi-monthly magazine containing news and reviews. It also produces *Poetry 0–16* and *Green Books for Children*.

Book Trust 45 East Hill, London, SW18 2QZ. Tel: 081 870 9055. It produces Parent Packs (0 to 5, 5 to 9 or 9 to 13s) providing regularly updated lists of recommended reading and other useful information. Send a large SAE and state which pack you require, quoting 'ref: LC'. The Trust also produces author profiles and lists of books for reluctant readers, multi-cultural links, etc. It helps organise Children's Book Week in November and oversees the excellent Children's Book of the Year publications.

Books for Your Children PO Box 507, Birmingham, B4 7TQ. Tel: 021 643 6411. Three magazines a year, linked to FCBG (see below).

Federation of Children's Book Groups Contact Alison Dick, 6 Bryce Place, Currie, Edinburgh, EH14 5LR. Tel: 031 449 2713. A parent-oriented network of regional groups. It runs an annual national conference, National Storytelling Week and administers the Children's Book of the Year Award (see below).

The Reading and Language Information Centre University of Reading, Bulmershe Court, Earley, Reading, GR6 1HY. Tel: 0734 318820 9–4 pm. Produces pamphlets and provides information for parents as well as teachers.

Useful books

Child Education (April) and *Junior Education* (October), Scholastic Publications. Monthly magazines for teachers, but these editions contain annual reviews of a whole range of children's books. *Junior Education* covers later Primary years.

Children's Book of the Year 1992 Selected and annotated by Julia Eccleshare. (For current information, contact Book Trust, see above.)

Good Book Guide Children's Books An annual supplement to the Good Book Guide. Contact the Good Book Guide, 91 Great Russell Street, London, WC1B 3PS. Tel: 071 580 8466.

Matching the Book to the Child Cliff Moon, Reading and Language Information Centre/WH Smith, 1993. A parent's guide to National Curriculum reading levels.

Special Needs Directory 1993/4 is prepared by the National Library for the Handicapped Child, with over 400 titles (literature for and about children with special needs, but useful to all) described, categorised and indexed. Free to parents. Contact Barnicoats, Parkengue, Penryn, Cornwall, TR10 9EP. Tel: 0326 372628.

Treasure Islands 2, Michael Rosen and Jill Burridge, BBC Books. An adult guide to children's writers and illustrators.

Children's book clubs

Books for Children PO Box 70, Cirencester, GL7 7AZ. Tel: 0793 420000. You must buy a number of titles in your first year of membership. Strong under-5s emphasis. Has an automatic book choice which must be cancelled by returning the order form.

Children's Book of the Month Club PO Box 199, Swindon, Wiltshire, SN3 BR. Tel: 0800 378 756. Similar to above: mostly hardback books. Age range 0–10, but three-quarters aimed at under-5s.

Letterbox Library Unit 2D, Leroy House, 136 Essex Road, London, N1 3QP. Tel: 071 226 1633. Specialises in non-sexist and multicultural books for all ages. Joining fee, four newsletters a year. You must buy three books in the first year.

Puffin Book Club Freepost, 27 Wrights Lane, London, W8 5BR. Tel: Freephone 0800 267888. This is a school-based scheme which has collective membership. Provides three separate book listings of Penguin material grouped by age. There are magazines for children with lively features, competitions, jokes, etc.

Red Fox Reader's Club A card-stamping scheme so you collect points every time you buy a title, or borrow one from the library. Once completed, your child becomes a member and is entitled to a free book. Contact Random House Children's Books Marketing Department, 20 Vauxhall Bridge Road, London, SW1V 2SA if you can't get hold of a card.

Red House The Red House, Witney, Oxford, OX8 5YF. Tel: 0993 771144. Like other postal book clubs, this offers good discounts. But unlike some, there is no annoying automatic selection to cancel. Usual opening offers and obligation to buy a number of books in your first year of membership. 13 newsletters a year with a good range for older children. Often includes a supplement focusing on educational books.

School Book Fairs 5 Airspeed Road, Priority Industrial Park, Christchurch, Dorset, BH23 4HD. Tel: 04252 79171. Organises book fairs in schools, concentrating on titles popular with children. Includes a good range of fiction, non-fiction, adventure, poetry, etc. listed in three reading ability ranges. Contact your school for details.

Computer aids

Better Books & Software, 3 Pagnal Drive, Dudley, DY1 4AZ. Tel: 0384 253276 for software relating to dyslexia.

Educational Software, a magazine produced twice a year, has current listings of language software programmes. Contact Rickett Educational Media, Great Western House, Langport, Somerset, TA10 9YU. Tel: 0458 253636.

Fun School (Europress) is good for general introduction skills. *Read Right Away* (HS Software), *Henrietta's Book of Spells* (Lander Software), *Fleet Street Phantom* (Sherston Software) and *Podd* (Applied Systems Knowledge) are popular. Sherston Software have a new 'talking books' range, linked with the Oxford Reading Tree, together with an entertaining programme *Sellardore tales* for older pupils with special needs.

Annual children's book awards

Best Books for Babies Award
Carnegie Medal
Children's Book Award (Mid-May; Titles are reviewed and chosen by children)
Emil/Kurt Maschler Award
Kate Greenaway Medal
Guardian Award for Children's Fiction
Macmillan Prize for a Children's Picture Book
The Mother Goose Award
Sheffield Children's Book Award
Signal Poetry for Children Award
Smarties Prize (includes a section of children's choices)

Times Educational Supplement Information Book Awards
Whitbread Children's Book Award

Organisations and projects dealing with language and/or home–school links

Advisory Centre for Education (ACE), 1B Aberdeen Studios, 22–24 Highbury Grove, London, N5 2AE. Tel: 071 354 8321 (2–5 pm). Free advice service and useful pamphlets.

Department for Education produces a free booklet *National School Tests in 1994* for parents (in several languages), aiming to clarify testing procedure. Contact DFE, Freepost 402, London, W1E 2DE. Tel: 0800 242323 9–6 pm Mon–Fri.

National Association for Primary Education Queen's Building, University of Leicester, Barrack Road, Northampton, NN2 6AF. Tel: 0604 363326. National and local groups focusing on effective policy and practice.

National Association for the Teaching of English Birley School Annexe, Fox Lane, Frecheville, Sheffield, S12 4WY. Tel: 0742 390081. A teacher's association mainly, but publishes some useful booklets on reading for parents.

National Confederation of Parent-Teacher Associations 2 Ebbsfleet Industrial Estate, Stonebridge Road, Gravesend, DA11 9DZ. Tel: 0474 560618. Aims to promote partnerships between home and school; also a good source of objective advice and can link parents with mutual needs.

National Literacy Trust Strand House, 7 Holbein Place, London, SW1 8NR. Tel: 071 828 2435. New umbrella organisation conducting research and aiming to promote good practice in literacy learning, establishing a data base of information.

Parents and Children and Teachers (PACT) Hackney Educational Psychology Services, Woodberry Down Centre, Woodberry Grove, London, N4 2SH. Tel: 081 809 7899. Project initially dealing with home–school reading programmes.

Organisations concerned with language learning difficulties and special needs

British Dyslexia Association 98 London Road, Reading, RG1 5AU. Tel: 0734 668271. Local support groups, help, advice, courses, etc.

The Dyslexia Institute 133 Gresham Road, Staines, Middlesex, TW18 2AJ. Tel: 0784 463851. Advice, assessments, specialist teaching.

Helen Arkell Centre Frensham, Farnham, Surrey, GU10 3BW. Tel: 0252 792400. Source of advice for professionals involved with dyslexics – can help parents too.

Hornsby Centre Glenshee Lodge, 261 Trinity Road, London SW18 3SN. Tel: 081 874 1844. See also book by Hornsby *Overcoming Dyslexia* Optima.

Whurr Publishers 19B Comton Terrace, London, N1 2UN. Tel: 071 359 5979. Source of books for children with dyslexia.

The Institute for Neuro-Physiological Psychology Warwick House, 4 Stanley Place, Chester, CH1 2LU. Tel: 0244 311414. Reflexology used to help children with reading difficulties.

The Irlen Centre 4 Moscow Mansions, 224 Cromwell Road,

London, SW6 0SP. Tel: 071 244 7099. Supplies colour overlays for children with reading discomfort.

National Deaf Children's Society (NDCS) 45 Hereford Road, London, W2 5AH. Tel: 071 229 9272/0800 252380 (1–5 pm) free-phone education helpline.

Partially Sighted Society Queen's Road, Doncaster, South Yorkshire, DN1 2NX. Tel: 0302 323132. Has three regional centres helping assess children and train and advise professionals.

Large Print Books Lythway, Windsor Bridge Road, Bath, BA2 3AX. Novels for 9+s.

Royal National Institute for the Blind (RNIB) 224 Great Portland Street, London W1N 6AA. Tel: 071 388 1266.

Dyspraxia Trust PO Box 30, Hitchin, Herts, SG5 1UU. Tel: 0462 454986. Contact for help regarding motor/learing difficulties.

Centre for Left-Handed Studies 43 Norwood Avenue, Didsbury, Manchester, M20 6EW. **Dextral Books** PO Box 52, Manchester M20 2PJ. Tel: 061 445 0159. Literature (*Left-Handed Helpline*, a guide which is good for handwriting tips) and equipment and a handwriting tutor list.

Handwriting Interest Group Contact Felicitie Barnes, 6 Fyfield Road, Ongar, Essex, CM5 0AH. Produces annual *Handwriting Review*. Beverly Scheib, 1 D'Abernon Drive, Stoke D'Abernon, Surrey, KT11 3JE, produces a leaflet for parents £2 & SAE.

Gifted Children's Information Centre Hampton Grange, 21 Hampton Lane, Solihull, Birmingham, B91 2QJ. Tel: 021 7054547. Specialises in helping gifted children who are left-handed and/or dyslexic.

Mensa Foundation for Gifted Children Mensa House, St John's Square, Wolverhampton, WV2 4AH. Tel: 0902 772771.

USEFUL ORGANISATIONS

National Association for Gifted Children Park Campus, Boughton Green Road, Northampton, NN2 7AL. Tel: 0604 792300.

Afro-Caribbean Education Resource Centre ACER Centre, Wyvil Road, London, SW8 2TJ. Provides information and publications.

Multilingual Matters Frankfurt Lodge, Clevedon Hall, Victoria Road, Clevendon, Avon, BS21 7SJ. Tel: 0275 876519. Produces four family newsletters a year.

Two-Tongue Tales Book Trust (see above). A dual language resource pack for 9–13 yrs.

Education Otherwise PO Box 120, Leamington Spa, Warwickshire, CV32 7ER. Tel: 0926 886828. Self-help network for parents educating their children at home.

Loans and resources

Clear Vision Loan Scheme Linden Lodge School, 61 Princes Way, London, SW19 6JB. Tel: 081 789 9575.

IBM Support Centre for People with Disabilities PO Box 31, Birmingham Road, Warwick, Warwickshire, CV34 5JL. Tel: 0800 269545.

National Association of Toy and Leisure Libraries (Play Matters) 68 Churchway, London, NW1 1LT. Tel: 071 387 9592. Toys, games, books and tapes, often particularly for children with special needs.

National Library for the Handicapped Child Wellington House, Wellington Road, Wokingham, Berks, RG11 2AG. Tel: 0734 891101.

National Listening Library Lant Street, London, SE1 1QK. Loans tapes from comprehensive reading list.

Useful books and materials

Reference and home learning for parents

Early aids for reading and writing

The Letterland ABC (book and tape available), the *Letterland Dictionary*, Letterland Storybooks (each focusing on a different Letterland phonic character) and *Reading and Writing with Letterland* (a useful Letterland parent's guide) gives a framework and ideas. Contact Letterland Direct Ltd, Freepost (KT4090), PO Box 161, Leatherhead, Surrey, KT22 8BR. Tel: 0372 360434 for mail order details.

First Steps to Reading (series), Usborne. Fun books packed with activities to share as well as offering first reading support.

Headstart, Hodder and Stoughton. A series running from pre-school to National Curriculum Key Stage 2. Good layout and notes for parents. Includes *Handwriting, Reading and writing* and *Spelling*.

Writestart, Living and Learning (Tel: 0223 357788). A package focusing on letter formation with activities for pencil control and some advice for parents.

Parent and Child, Reed Children's Books. Six graded sets from

USEFUL BOOKS AND MATERIALS

board books to books for nine-year-olds. Clear and easy to follow.

Reading games, You and Your Child series, Usborne, 1993. How to make easy, fun games.

I Spy ABC, Sally Anne Lambert, Picturemac.

From Acorn to Zoo, Satoshi Kitamura, Red Fox.

A was Once an Apple Pie, Edward Lear and Julia Lacome, Walker.

Amazing Alphabets, Lisa Bruce and Debi Gliori, Frances Lincoln.

The Usborne Book of First Words, ill. Sue Stitt, Usborne.

My First Word Book, Angela Wilkes, Dorling Kindersley.

My First Dictionary, Betty Root, Dorling Kindersley.

Games

Big Alphabet Card Game, *What Am I?* (Listening game), Early Learning Centre.

I Spy, *Noah's Ark Memory Game*, *Tongue Twisters* (initial sounds listening game) all from Living and Learning (Tel: 0223 357788).

a b c game (Ravensburger) and *Spell and learn* (Playground) are nice matching games.

First Word/Alphabet Jigcards (Boots).

Usborne Picture Word Lotto (two ability levels).

Professor ABC (Texas Instruments) (portable, entertaining way to practise skills).

Older reference resources

See Headstart and Parent and Child ranges above.

Wordmasters (series), George Beal and William Edmonds, Kingfisher. Lively and child-friendly, coverage includes: *Proverbs*, *Good grammar* and *A First Thesaurus*.

Oxford Junior Dictionary. Oxford have just revised their dictionary range, from *My First Oxford Dictionary* (5+), the *Illustrated Junior Dictionary* (7+) to *The Oxford Primary School Dictionary*.

Grammar Puzzles and *Spelling Puzzles*, Usborne English Skills. Popular with kids.

Ginn Workbooks (WH Smith) cover phonics, spelling and handwriting from 5–7, then grammar and punctuation from 7–9 and from 9–11.

Test Your Child's Spelling and *Test Your Child's Spelling Practice*, Hodder and Stoughton. No frills!

Word search, *Crosswords*, Early Learning Centre.
Also, the Ladybird Word Games series, with child-catching titles like *Wild Word Search*. 'adybird also has Fun, Practise and Test Your Child series, with increasingly serious formats!

Essential for English (series), Scholastic. Has some titles suitable for home use such as *Initial letter sounds* and *Reading for Information*. *Spelling*, in the Bright Ideas range, is also loaded with practical suggestions.

Games

(See above also)

Spell and Learn, Early Learning Centre. A word-building game.

Junior Boggle, *Boggle*, Parker. Word-building against the clock.

Junior Scrabble.

Never-Ending Stories, Living and Learning or Early Learning Centre. A creative story sequence game.

Word Pool, Early Learning Centre. A board/dice game where you 'hop' for letters to make a word.

Ravensburger Memory games, including *Dinosaur*, *Disney* and *First Memory*.

Letter tiles or magnetic letters for your own word games, messages, etc., Early Learning Centre.

Super Speak & Spell, Texas Instruments. 6–11 yrs electronic spelling games.

Making Books

A Book of One's Own, Paul Johnson, Hodder and Stoughton. Inspiration for parents.

How to Draw Lettering, Cartoons, both in Usborne series. Good
for older children, as is *The Usborne Book of Pop-Ups*.
How to Make Pop-Up Birthday/Thank You, etc. Cards, Kingfisher.
Creative calligraphby, Peter Halide, Kingfisher.

Look out for a bookmaking book for children by Kingfisher
due out later in 1994.

Tempting texts to share together

This list offers examples of entertaining books set out in sections to
make them easier to use. However, these sections are not mutually
exclusive. So, for example, a book under 'reluctant reader' can be
enjoyed by anyone, and a reluctant reader may be charmed by
books on the 'picture books for older readers' listing. It is simply a
matter of emphasis. All the titles aim at popular appeal but I have
omitted the big three (Dahl, Blyton and King-Smith) and children's
classics as you and your child are already familiar with these. There
are however two classic series worth nothing:

Little Greats from Random House, offers 20 classic picture books
in affordable hardback. Titles include *Whistle for Willie* by Ezra
Jack Keats, *Dogger* by Shirley Hughes and three gems from Pat
Hutchins: *Goodnight Owl!*, *Titch* and *Rosie's Walk*.

Puffin Modern Classics offers a wide range of proven quality titles
in smart packaging. Titles include *The Mouse and his Child* by
Russell Hoban, *Tom's Midnight garden* by Philippa Pearce and *A
Wizard of Earthsea* by Ursula Le Guin.

Why are the lists so long?

I want to offer as wide a selection as possible of popular texts for
you to explore with your child. My research has included experts
from the book world, teachers, librarians and parents. But most of
all I have tried to reflect what children themselves enjoy reading.

The lists are written more or less in order of difficulty — the easiest books first.

Starting simply — for sharing with pre-schoolers and using later for early reading

Where's Billy?, Martha Alexander, Walker Books.

Duck, Puppy (Match and Patch series), Opal Dunn, Doubleday, 1992/3.

Teddy Bear Teddy Bear, Carol Lawson, David Bennett paperbacks.

Young Joe, Reading, Jan Omerod, Walker Books.

A Fox Got My Socks, Hilda Offen, Red Fox, 1994.

Four Fierce Kittens, Joyce Dunbar and Jakki Wood, Orchard Books, 1991.

Bathwater's Hot, *Noisy*, Shirley Hughes, Sainsbury/Walker.

Just Like Jasper, *Jasper's Beanstalk*, Mick Inkpen, Picture Knight/ Hodder and Stoughton.

Ladybird Moves Home, Richard Fowler, Doubleday, 1993.

Simpkin, Quentin Blake, Jonathan Cape, 1993.

Who Sank the Boat? Pamela Allan, Picture Puffin.

Do You Dare? Paul and Emma Rogers and Sonia Holleyman, Orchard.

We're Going on a Bear Hunt, Michel Rosen and Helen Oxenbury, Walker Books.

Five Minutes Peace/Peace at Last, Jill Murphy, Walker/PictureMac.

Picture books to share with younger readers

Cockatoos, Quentin Blake, Red Fox, 1994.

Mrs Armitage on Wheels, Quentin Blake, Picture Lions, 1990.

The Park in the Dark, Martin Waddell and Barbara Firth, Walker Books.

Owl Babies, Martin Waddell and Patrick Benson, Walker Books, 1993.

After the Storm, Nick Butterworth, Picture Lions, 1993.

Winnie the Witch, Korky Paul and Valerie Thomas, OUP, 1987.

A Dark, Dark Tale, Ruth Brown, Red Fox, 1992.

The Bear Under The Stairs, Helen Cooper, Doubleday, 1993.

Sally and the Limpet, *My Friend Whale*, Simon James, Walker Books.

Snowy, Berlie Doherty and Keith Bowen, Picture Lions, 1992.

The Brave Hare, Dave and Julie Saunders, Frances Lincoln, 1993.

Kipper, *Penguin Small*, *Lullabyhullaballoo*, Mick Inkpen, Picture Knight/Hodder and Stoughton.

Picture books for older children

NB The previous section is also relevant.

The Jolly Christmas Postman, Janet and Allan Ahlberg, Heinemann, 1991.

Hue Boy, Rita Phillips Mitchell and Caroline Binch, Gollancz, 1992.

Amazing Grace, Mary Hoffman and Caroline Binch, Frances Lincoln, 1991.

Gregory Cool, Caroline Binch, Frances Lincoln, 1994.

No Problem, Eileen Browne and David Parkins, Walker Books, 1993.

Moving, Michael Rosen and Sophy Williams, Viking, 1993.

Willy and Hugh, *Zoo*, Anthony Browne, Red Fox/Julia MacRae.

The Night Shimmy, Anthony Browne and Gwen Straus, Red Fox.

The Hidden House, Martin Waddell and Angela Barrett, Walker Books.

One World, Michael Foreman, Red Fox.

The Orphan Boy, Tololwa M. Molle/Paul Morin, OUP.

At the Crossroads, Rachel Isadora, Red Fox.

Jackdaw, Ann and Reg Cartwright, Hutchinson, 1993.

A Fairy Tale, Tony Ross, Red Fox, 1993.

Brother Eagle, Sister Sky, Susan Jeffers, Picture Puffin, 1993.

War Game, Michael Foreman, Pavilion, 1993.

The Paperbag Prince, Colin Thompson, Red Fox, 1994.

The Man, Raymond Briggs, Julia MacRae, 1992.

It Was a Dark and Stormy Night, Janet and Allan Ahlberg, Viking, 1993.

Time and the Clockmice Etcetera, Peter Dickenson and Emma Cichester, Clark Doubleday.

Books without words or largely for looking

Not a Worry in the World, Monica Williams, Walker, 1992.

The Great Escape, *Our House on the Hill*, Philippe Dupasquier, Walker/Picture Puffin.

Window, Jeannie Baker, Red Fox.

Imagine, Alison Lester, Picture Puffin.

Full Moon Soup, Alistar Graham, David Bennett.

Where's Wally? series, Martin Handford, Walker Books.

Going West, Martin Waddell and Philippe Dupasquier, Picture Puffin.

Reluctant readers – picture appeal

(See above, too.)

The Wacky Book of Witches, Annie Civardi and Graham Philpot, David Bennett.

The Happy Rag, Tony Ross, Red Fox.

Changes, *The Tunnel*, Anthony Browne, Walker Books.

Berenstain Bears series, Stan and Jan Berenstain, Beginner Books.

The Kettleship Pirates, Rodney Peppe, Picture Puffin.

Funnybone series, Allan Ahlberg and Andre Amstutz, Little Mammoth.

The World that Jack Built, Ruth Brown, Red Fox.

Little Dracula series, Martin Waddell and Joseph Wright, Walker Books.

Dr Xargle's series, Jeanne Willis and Tony Ross, Red Fox.

Sanji and the Baker, Robin Tzannes and Korky Paul, OUP, 1993.

Stanley Bagshaw series, Bob Wilson, Picture Puffin.

The Chocolate Wedding, Posy Simmonds, Picture Puffin, 1993.

Asterix series, R Goscinny and A Uderzo, Hodder and Stoughton.

The Planet of Terror (adventure game series), Patrick Burston and Alastair Graham, Walker.

USEFUL BOOKS AND MATERIALS

Agent Arthur, Usborne Puzzle Adventures, Usborne.

The True Story of the Three Little Pigs!, *The Stinky Cheese Man and Other Fairly Stupid Tales*, Jon Scieszka and Lane Smith, Picture Puffin.

The Frog Prince Continued, Jon Scieszka and Steve Johnson, Picture Puffin.

The Dog that Dug, Jonathan Long and Korky Paul, Red Fox, 1993.

If Dinosaurs Came to Town, Dom Mansell, David Bennett.

The Ankle Grabber, etc. (Creepies series), Rose Impey and Moira Kemp, Young Lions.

Look out for graphic novels such as *Orson Cart* series, Steve Donald, Red Fox. Also see Raymond Briggs, Phillip Pullman and Mark Foster books.

Serious about series – progressive

Some children love the support that a series gives, others find them intimidating. Watch out for entertaining authors.

Red nose readers series, Walker:

Allan Ahlberg and Colin McNaughton (beginners' fun).

Animal Crackers series, Orchard Books:

Rose Impey and Shoo Rayner.

Ready, steady, read!, Puffin:

The Lucky Duck Song, Martin Waddell and Judy Brown.
Cyril's Cat, *Charlie's Night Out*, Shoo Rayner.

Kingfisher:

Robbers and Witches, *Feathery Furry Tales*, Judy Hindley and Toni Goffe.

Flippers:

Sir Cumference and Clever Dick, *Sir Cumference and Little Daisy*, John Ryan.
Clever Clive, *Loopy Lucy*, Joan Lingard and Jacqui Thomas.
Maisy in the Mud, *Maisy's Masterpiece*, Sheila Lavelle.

Jets series, Young Lions:

Jessie Runs Away, Rachael Anderson.
Grubble Trouble, Hilda Offen.
Martians at Mudpuddle Farm, Michael Morpurgo and Shoo Rayner.
Harry Moves House, Chris Powling and Scoular Anderson.
Monty, The Dog Who Wears Glasses, Colin West.

Cartwheels series:

Blessu, Dick King-Smith.

Banana Books, Heinemann:

The Breadwitch, Jenny Nimmo.
The Dognapper, Sheila Lavelle.
Scaredy-Cat, Anne Fine.
Freckle Juice, Judy Blume.
Deadly Friend, Jamila Gavin.
Snakes & Ladders, Michael Morpurgo.
Storm, Kevin Crossley-Holland.

Jumbo Jets:

Forecast of Fear, Keith Brumpton.
Fergus the Forgetful, Margaret Ryan.

USEFUL BOOKS AND MATERIALS

Superchamp books, Heinemann:

Size Twelve, Robert Westall.

Blackie Snappers:

The Saturday Knight, Margaret Ryan.
The Revolting Baby, Mary Hooper.

Keeping going – easily entertaining and increasing words

Jolly Roger, Who's That Banging on the Ceiling? (Crazy poems),
  Colin McNaughton, Walker Books.
Dilly the Dinosaur series, Tony Bradman and Susan Hellard,
  Mammoth.
Bill's New Frock, Anne Fine, Mammoth.
Wonderful Robert and Sweetie-Pie Nell, Diana Hendry, Walker.
The Not-So-Jolly Roger (Time Warp Trio), Jon Scieszka and Lane
  Smith, Puffin.
Count Karlstein, Philip Pullman, Yearling.
Amber Brown is not a Crayon, Paula Danziger, Mammoth.
The Big Goal sport series, Rob Child, Young Corgi.
Dog Bites Goalie & Other Soccer Stories, Michael Hardcastle,
  Mammoth.
Ms Wiz series, Terence Blacker and Kate Simpson, Young Piper.
Black Woolly Pony, White Chalk Horse, Jane Gardam, Walker.
The Angel of Nitshill Road, Anne Fine, Mammoth.
Your Guess is as Good as Mine, Bernard Ashley, Young Corgi.
The Enchanted Horse, Josie Smith series, Magdalen Nabb, Young
  Lion.
Dockside School Stories, Bernard Ashley, Walker Doubles.
Sam, the Girl Detective series, Tony Bradman, Yearling.
Flat Stanley and Other Adventures, Jeff Brown and Tomi Ungerer,
  Mammoth.
The Real Tilly Beany, Annie Dalton, Mammoth.

The Tree House, Gillian Cross and Paul Howard, Methuen.

Bubble Trouble, Margaret Mahy and Tony Ross, Hamish Hamilton.

The Suitcase Kid, The Story of Tracy Beaker, The Mum Minder, Jacquine Wilson, Yearling/Doubleday.

Paper Faces, Rachel Anderson, Lions.

Harvey Angell, Diana Hendry, Red Fox.

Two Weeks with the Queen, Morris Gleitzman, Piper.

Gobbo the Great, Gillian Cross, Mammoth.

Wizard in the Woods, Jean Ure, Walker.

The Zarnia Experiment series, Robert Leeson, Mammoth.

Grandpa Chatterji, Jamila Gavin, Methuen.

The Exiles, Hilary McKay, Lions.

Krindlekrax, Philip Ridley, Red Fox.

Unreal!, Unbelievable! (short stories with a twist), Paul Jennings, Puffin.

Older entertaining and more demanding reads

Between the Moon and the Rock, Judy Allan, Julia MacRae.

Ghostly Companions and *The Face at the Window*, Vivian Alcock, Mammoth/Methuen.

Hacker, Malorie Blackman, Corgi.

The Great Elephant Chase, Gillian Cross, OUP.

Everyone Else's Parents Said Yes!, Paula Danziger, Piper.

The House of Rats, Stephen Elboz, OUP.

Flour Babies, Anne Fine, Hamish Hamilton.

Redwall, Salamandastron, Brian Jaques, Red Fox.

But Can the Phoenix Sing?, Christa Laird, Julia MacRae.

Kiss the Dust, Elizabeth Laird, Mammoth.

Underrunners, Margaret Mahy, Hamish Hamilton.

Low Tide, William Mayne, Red Fox.

My Friend Walter, Waiting for Anya, Michael Morpurgo, Mammoth.

The Snow Spider, UltraMarine, Jenny Nimmo, Mammoth.

Vote for Baz, Ann Pilling, Puffin.

USEFUL BOOKS AND MATERIALS

Truckers (trilogy), Terry Pratchett, Corgi.

Along a Lonely Road, Catherine Sefton, Hamish Hamilton.

Riding the Wales, Theresa Tomlinson, Walker.

Tomorrow is a Stranger, Geoffrey Trease, Piper.

Pigeon Summer, Ann Turnbull, Walker.

The Flawed Glass, Ian Strachan, Mammoth.

The Vandemark Mummy, *Tillerman Saga* series, Cynthia Voigt, Lions.

Gulf, The Kingdom by the Sea, Robert Westall, Mammoth.

Poetry selections – a few examples

The Kingfisher Nursery and Playtime series has many useful titles such as *ABCs and other Learning Rhymes* and *Clapping Rhymes*.

Pudding and Pie, Oranges and Lemons, Ian Beck, OUP.

Out and About, Shirley Hughes, Walker.

A Very First Poetry Book, Another Very First Poetry Book, John Foster, OUP.

Fifteen Ways to Get Dressed, Kathy Henderson, Frances Lincoln.

Riddling Rhymes for Small Children, Delphine Evans, Beaver Books.

A Cup of Starshine, Jill Bennett and Graham Percy, Walker.

I Din Do Nuttin and other poems, John Agard, Red Fox.

Dinosaur Poems, John Foster and Korky Paul, OUP.

Say it Again Granny!, John Agard, Little Mammoth.

Don't Put Mustard in the Custard, Michael Rosen and Quentin Blake, Picture Lions.

Algernon and other Cautionary Tales, Hilaire Belloc and Quentin Blake, Red Fox.

Please Mrs Butler, Allan Ahlberg, Puffin.

Smile Please! Tony Bradman, Puffin.

Gargling with Jelly, Brian Patten, Puffin.

No Hickory No Dickory No Dock, John Agard and Grace Nichols, Young Puffin.

Early in the Morning, Charles Causley, Puffin.

An Imaginary Menagerie, Roger McGough and Tony Blundell, Puffin.

A Stack of Story Poems, Tony Bradman (selected by), Corgi.

All Change, Libby Houston, OUP.

Chasing the Sun, Sally Bacon (compiler), Simon & Schuster.

The Kingfisher Book of Children's Poetry, Comic Verse, M Rosen and R McGough.

Story collections to read aloud

The Kingfisher Nursery Collection, Sally Emerson and Susan Price, C and M Maclean.

The Orchard Book of Nursery Stories, Sophie Windham, Orchard Paperback, 1993.

The Bedtime Book, selected by Kathy Henderson/Penny Ives ill., Frances Lincoln, 1992.

Teddy Tales, Sally Grindley and Peter Utton, Orchard Books, 1993.

Round About Six, Kaye Webb (selected by), Frances Lincoln, 1992.

Time for Telling (world-wide stories), Mary Medlicott and Sue Williams, Kingfisher, 1991.

Dinosaur Superstar (Readathon), Toni Goffe (ill.), Knight, 1992.

The Orchard Book of Fairy Tales, Rose Impey and Ian Beck, Orchard Books.

What's For Dinner and other stories, Jacqui Thomas (ill.), Knight Books, 1993.

Fantastic Stories, Terry Jones and Michael Foreman, Pavilion, 1992.

The Cloth of Dreams, Sally Grindley (ed.) and James Mayhew, Little Brown, 1992.

Stories by Firelight, Shirley Hughes, Bodley Head, 1993.

Horse & Pony Stories, Christine Pullein-Thompson, Kingfisher.

Funny Stories/Science Fiction Stories, M Rosen/Edward Blishen, Kingfisher Story Library.

The Orchard Book of Magical Tales, Margaret Mayo and Jane Ray, Orchard, 1993.

Shark and Chips and other stories, Puffin Book Club, Puffin, 1992.

Realms of Gold Myths and Legends, Ann Pilling and Kady Mac-Donald Denton, Kingfisher, 1993.

The Oxford Book of Scarrytales, Dennis Pepper, OUP.

The Orchard Book of Greek Myths, Geraldine McCaughrean and Emma Chichester Clark, Orchard.

Koshka's Tales, James Mayhew, Kingfisher, 1993.

Tales for the Telling, Edna O'Brien and Michael Foreman, Puffin, 1988.

Stories from Firefly Island, Benedict Blathwayt, Julia MacRae, 1992.

The Arabia Nights, Brian Alderson and Michael Foreman, Victor Gollancz.

Mouth Open, Story Jump Out, Grace Hallworth, Mammoth.

Early Magic, Sky Magic, Rosalind Kerven, Cambridge, 1991.

Children's Classics to Read Aloud, Edward Blishen, Kingfisher, 1991.

Good Sports! A Bag of Sports Stories, Tony Bradman (ed.), Doubleday, 1992.

I Like This Story (50 classic tasters, if you don't mind snippets), Kaye Webb, Puffin.

Tempting tapes

Many libraries have good audio selections and will give you some idea of the range available. This list aims to provide ideas for older listeners and readers too.

A Day of Rhymes, Sarah Pooley, Tellastory.

Rosie and Jim Stories, John Cunliffe, Tempo Children's Classics.

Naughty Bear Stories including *Ruby, Bad Mood Bear*, etc., read by Felicity Kendall, Tellastory.

Katie Morag and the Two Grandmothers, Marie Hedderwick and Bill Torrance, Collins Audio.

Meg and Mog, Helen Nicoll, read by Maureen Lipman, Cover-to-Cover.

Jolly Snow and Other Stories, Jane Hissey, read by Anton Rogers, Tellastory.

HELP YOUR CHILD WITH READING AND WRITING

After the Storm, One Snowy Night, Nick Butterworth, read by Richard Briars, Collins Audio.

Hairy MacLary, Lynly Dodd, read by Tom Conti, BBC.

The Owl who was Afraid of the Dark, Tomlinson, read by Maureen Lipman, Cover-to-Cover.

Happy Families, Allan Ahlberg, read by Martin Jarvis, Cover-to-Cover.

Aladdin, Pinocchio, Beauty and the Beast, etc. (Disney films), Pickwick Group.

Stanley Bagshaw (four stories), Bob Wilson, Cover-to-Cover.

Magical Stories, Chris Powling (compiled), Collins Audio.

Non-stop Nonsense, Margaret Mahy, read by Tony Robinson, Chivers/Cavalcade.

The Animals of Farthing Wood, BBC.

The Wind in the Willows, Kenneth Graham, multi-voiced, Tempo Children's Classics.

Crummy Mummy and Me, Anne Fine, Cover-to-Cover.

Mystery Stories, Tony Bradman (compiled), Collins Audio.

Tin-Tin, BBC.

True Ghost Stories, read by Richard O'Brien, Collins Audio.

Krindlekrax, Philip Ridley, read by Rik Mayall, Tellastory.

Truckers (trilogy), Terry Pratchett, read by Tony Robinson, Corgi.

The Man, Raymond Briggs, read by Michael Palin, Tellastory.

The Ghost of Thomas Kempe, Penelope Lively, Cover-to-Cover.

Redwall, Brian Jacques, Tellastory.

The 12th Day of July, Across the Barricades, Joan Lingard, Cover-to-Cover.

As seen on TV!

It's a real chicken and egg case with so-called media tie-ins! Which came first, the fame of Jane Hissey (*Little Bear*, Red Fox), of *Five Children and It* (E Nesbitt, Puffin), of the Josie Smith series (Magdalen Nabb, Young Lions) or their success on the box? From the

USEFUL BOOKS AND MATERIALS

Crystal Maze adventures to *Pingu*, from *Rosie and Jim* to *Ghost-writer*, there will be books and comics to tempt young viewers to turn to print. These books tend to come in several forms so it's worth hunting for one which suits your child's reading level. For example, Ladybird do lively versions of Disney films such as Aladdin in about seven formats, including Read-By-Myself Tales, Read-To-Me and Classic large book size which is useful for shared story-reading. If you take just one blockbuster like *The Animals of Farthing Wood* by Colin Dann, there will be a huge array of books based on it as well as complete novels.

If your child gets hooked on a programme or film it's worth contacting the television company or a good bookseller to find out if there are books available. Book Clubs also need to have a keen eye on popular trends and so may offer titles which match up with viewing patterns. The following list gives some examples, although the heroes and heroines of the silver screen can fade fast. It is real books like Mary Norton's *The Borrowers* series which have enduring appeal.

Younger series include:

   Pingu, *Spot*, *Postman Pat*, *Thomas the Tank Engine*, *Rosie and Jim*, *Noddy*, Beatrix Potter stories and *Funnybones*.

Older series and films include:

   Woof! (Fantail), *Thunderbirds* (Young Corgi), *Desperate Dan* (Ladybird), *Captain Scarlet*, *Indianna Jones*, Disney Classics, *Ghostwriter* (Bantam), *Truckers*, *The Secret Garden* (Frances Hodgson Burnett) and *Madame Doubtfire* (Anne Fine).

INDEX